D1527856

Maynooth Studies in Irish Local History

SERIES EDITOR   Raymond Gillespie

This is one of six new pamphlets in the Maynooth Studies in Irish Local History Series to be published in the year 2000. Like their predecessors, most of the pamphlets are based on theses completed as part of the M.A. in local history programme in National University of Ireland, Maynooth. While the regions and time span which they cover are diverse, from Waterford to Monaghan, and from the fourteenth to the twentieth centuries, they all share a conviction that the exploration of the local past can shed light on the evolution of modern societies. They each demonstrate that understanding the evolution of local societies is important. The local worlds of Ireland in the past are as complex and sophisticated as the national framework in which they are set. The communities which peopled those local worlds, whether they be the inhabitants of religious houses, industrial villages or rural parishes, shaped and were shaped by their environments to create a series of interlocking worlds of considerable complexity. Those past worlds are best interpreted not through local administrative divisions, such as the county, but in human units: local places where communities of people lived and died. Untangling what held these communities together, and what drove them apart, gives us new insights into the world we have lost.

These pamphlets each make a significant contribution to understanding Irish society in the past. Together with twenty-eight earlier works in this series they explore something of the hopes and fears of those who lived in Irish local communities in the past. In doing so they provide examples of the practice of local history at its best and show the vibrant discipline which the study of local history in Ireland has become in recent years.

Maynooth Studies in Irish Local History: Number 33

Portlaw, county Waterford
1825–76

Portrait of an industrial village
and its cotton industry

Tom Hunt

IRISH ACADEMIC PRESS
DUBLIN • PORTLAND, OR

First published in 2000 by
IRISH ACADEMIC PRESS
44, Northumberland Road, Dublin 4, Ireland
and in the United States of America by
IRISH ACADEMIC PRESS
c/o ISBS, 5804 NE Hassalo Street, Portland, OR 97213–3644.

website: www.iap.ie

British Library Cataloguing in Publication Data
Hunt, Tom
    Portlaw, County Waterford, 1825–76 : portrait of an industrial village and its
    cotton industry. – (Maynooth studies in Irish local history; no. 33)
    1. Cotton manufacture – Ireland – Portlaw – History – 19th century 2. Portlaw
    (Ireland) – History – 19th century 3. Portlaw (Ireland) – Economic conditions –
    19th century
    I. Title
    941.9'081

    ISBN 0–7165–2722–7

Library of Congress Cataloging-in-Publication Data
Hunt, Tom.
    Portlaw, county Waterford, 1825–76: portrait of an industrial village and its
    cotton industry / Tom Hunt.
        p. cm.—(Maynooth studies in local history; no. 33)
    ISBN 0–7165–2722–7 (pbk)
        1. Portlaw (Ireland)—History. 2. Cotton trade—Ireland—Portlaw—History—
    19th century. 3. Industries—Ireland—Portlaw—History—19th century. I. Title.
    II. Series.

    DA995.P67 H86 2000
    941.9'1–dc21   00–044841

Typeset in 10 pt on 12 pt Bembo by
Carrigboy Typesetting Services, County Cork
Printed by ColourBooks Ltd., Dublin

Contents

Acknowledgements

In the research and writing of this work I have been facilitated by a great many individuals and institutions. For their helpful and courteous assistance, I would like to express my thanks and appreciation to the staffs of the National Library of Ireland; the National Archives of Ireland; the library, N.U.I., Maynooth; the Waterford room of the Municipal Library, Waterford; the library of the Society of Friends, Swanbrook House, Dublin; the Valuation Office; the Registry of Deeds and the Westmeath County Library.

Dr Raymond Gillespie provided the inspirational teaching. The advice, comments and guidance of Dr Jacinta Prunty were invaluable.

The support and friendship of my fellow students in the Maynooth M.A. class of 1997–9 was especially appreciated.

My teaching colleagues, Anne Hanly and Felicity English, were always generous with help and advice when required on computer related difficulties. Pearly Tanner and Sheila Keenan also provided computer expertise.

Portlaw local historian Willie Power and Waterford historian Bill Irish were equally generous with their time and material.

My final and greatest debt is to my wife, Mary, who both understood my fascination with the world of Portlaw and the Malcomsons and was supportive and patient throughout the months of research and writing.

Introduction

Portlaw, county Waterford, is located in the parish of Clonagam, in the barony of Upperthird, approximately eleven miles from Waterford city and five miles from Carrick-on-Suir. The river Clodiagh flows through the village which is located roughly two miles from the river Suir. Figure 1 provides an 1840s view of the district. In the nineteenth century, the most successful Irish attempt at establishing a cotton industry, employing more than 1,600 people at its peak was centered on the village. The industry also determined the evolution of the village through the mid nineteenth century.

In general terms this study investigates how the industrial revolution, impacted at the local level, by examining the growth and development of the cotton industry at Portlaw. The study concentrates on three main themes. The original physical structure of the industrial village and the dramatic redevelopment of the town in the late 1850s and early 1860s is investigated. Paternalism

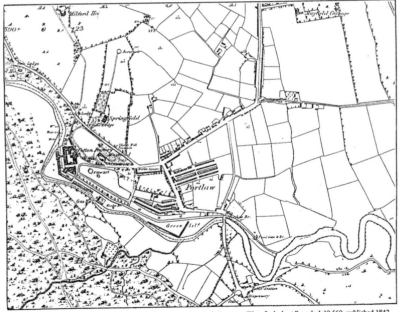

Source: O.S., county Waterford, sheet 8, scale 1:10,560, published 1842.

1. Portlaw O.S. map 1841

and the Quaker concern for the welfare and well-being of the factory operatives allied to the desire to produce an efficient and dependable work-force influenced the development of a range of social institutions. These are described and their impact on the quality of life in the village assessed. The third major theme concentrates on an examination of the factory infra-structure and analyses the factory performance over the period of study, investigating the processes involved in transforming raw cotton to the finished article, market developments and changes in the labour force and structure. Throughout the study, a context is established by comparing developments at Portlaw to happenings at the national level.

The Malcomson family and their contribution to the primary, secondary and tertiary sectors of the nineteenth-century Irish economy have received little historical attention. Cormac Ó Gráda is the only historian to grant the family more than passing mention in a general work.[1] Margaret Fogarty, in her 1968 thesis, examined the impact of the family on the economic development of the lower Suir valley. The Portlaw cotton plant is the centerpiece of this study with the Clonmel milling business and the Waterford shipping interests also evaluated. This work is heavily influenced by the Malcomson family memoirs but was written at a time when certain primary sources were unavailable or inaccessible.[2] Majella Walsh's 1995 thesis, 'Portlaw, a model industrial village' is an architectural history of the town featuring a com-prehensive inventory of the town's buildings accompanied by detailed drawings and illustrations. The author recognises the mid-nineteenth century remodelling of the village but places the development a decade earlier than this study.[3] A.P Williamson, in an article dealing with the impact of Quakers on the Irish textile industry examined the Malcomson contribution to the development of Portlaw and speculated on some of the possible formative influences on their social policies. However Williamson wrote from the belief that the town in its present form was the original development and was apparently unaware of the mid-century remodelling.[4] Desmond G. Neill wrote from the same perspective and was also heavily influenced by the family memoir.[5] An article written in 1910 included a mixture of contemporary reportage, folklore and historical fact in which the main emphasis is on the physical structure of the Portlaw factory.[6] One comment by the author is apt and provides an appro-riate summary on the current state of Malcomson historiography. He found 'it very strange that none of our country historians has gone to the trouble of investigating the story of the great Portlaw industry, one of the most interesting things of its day in Ireland'.[7]

Denis Macneice has pioneered the study of Irish industrial villages concentrating on developments in Ulster. His 1981 thesis focussed on the quality of housing built for workers in six Ulster industrial villages, examining their structure, size, extent of accommodation and sanitary facilities.[8] The standard of housing was compared with the general standard of working class housing in other areas of the United Kingdom. In a later article, the 1830s village of Gilford is studied in depth.[9] The mill housing, built by McMaster and Company was grafted onto the existing village and much of the social structures and community facilities that developed were remarkably similar to the developments at Portlaw.

An eclectic range of sources were used in the compilation of this essay including parliamentary papers, private papers, newspaper reports, material produced by government agencies and a variety of contemporary printed accounts. A major difficulty was the absence of a comprehensive collection of accounts. The only surviving business accounts of the firm relate to the 1830s.[10] It is difficult to establish how comprehensive these are but they contain useful information on the trade connections of the firm at this time. The Malcomson family papers available in the National Archives are particularly useful. These are included in the Hardman, Winder and Stokes papers and consist of a number of large boxes of material dealing with the affairs of the family.[11] These contain a comprehensive collection of personal papers including wills, marriage agreements and other material of a similar nature. A second body of papers deals with the problems that developed in 1870 when Mrs Nannie Malcomson, widow of Joseph Malcomson and testamentary guardian of her son, Joseph, 'a minor,' applied to have her son's share of almost £200,000 withdrawn from the firm. A third section deals with some of the business dealings of the family firm including the legal papers relating to the bankruptcy of the firm in 1876.

Parliamentary papers include the reports of the inspectors of factories published annually between 1835–8 and biannually between 1838–77. This inspectorate was established to ensure that new factory regulations, particularly those pertaining to age and education of workers, were being observed. The cotton factory at Portlaw was inspected regularly and often singled out for special mention. The reports help to form a more complete picture of internal factory conditions with a focus on the workers and their welfare. The inspectors of factories also compiled at irregular intervals returns of the numbers employed in the factories subject to inspection. Between 1836 and 1875, nine different sets of statistical returns were made to parliament detailing the numbers of employees, their age and gender structure as well as the number of working mills and weaving factories. As the sole official source of employment figures they were invaluable in examining the employment history of the firm. The weakness of the returns is their irregular nature; being non-consecutive they lack the value of a continuous annual series.

Material compiled by government agencies provided the major sources for reconstructing the historical geography of the village. The six inch ordnance survey maps of 1842[12] and 1907,[13] highlighting the transformation in morphology, provide a framework for the study. These maps represent a snapshot of the area at the time of survey. The changes that took place between the publication of the first ordnance survey maps and the later edition of 1907 were identified by using the undated field-maps of the valuation office. Changes were recorded at each period of valuation on these maps, making it possible to map the town at different stages of its development. Significant detail on the timing of the changes was extracted from the accompanying cancellation books of the valuation office.[14] The field book,[15] perambulation book[16] and house books[17] used by Richard Griffith's valuators as they compiled information for the printed valuation of 1850 were a most important source for the reconstruction of the tenurial and architectural history of the town and its geography pre-1850.

A 1930s family memoir entitled *Notes on the Malcomson family*,[18] is a useful guide to the Malcomson family and establishes a chronology for many of their business ventures. The memoir is a valuable resource for a range of primary documents which are not available elsewhere, including extracts from inventories, letter books, depositions to parliament and extracts from accounts.

Several newspapers covered the affairs of nineteenth-century Waterford. *The Waterford Mail* published a number of detailed descriptive features on the workings of the cotton factory. The paper is particularly useful in the 1860s, reporting on meetings of societies such as the literary and debating society and the local agricultural society. Reports of the addresses delivered to meetings of these societies contain valuable insights into the attitudes and philosophies of key figures in developments of the town. The *Waterford Newsletter*, 'a cornucopia of information about Waterford's trade',[19] was used to quantify the imports and exports of cotton, by the Malcomson firm. This was a trade paper published three times weekly between 1836 and 1917, but unfortunately no issues survive for the period 1849–68. It identified ships arriving and departing from the port of Waterford and listed their cargoes and the name of the importing or exporting firm. This range of sources allows scope to reconstruct many aspects of the history of a nineteenth-century Irish industrial community.

From rural cluster to planned industrial village

Portlaw, situated at the entrance to the Curraghmore demesne of the marquis of Waterford has the locational characteristics of a landlord created estate village, a familiar feature in the Irish urban landscape. However, it is not a typical estate village. Portlaw is a rare south of Ireland example of a purpose built industrial village, owing its origin, growth and development to the initiative of various members of the Malcomson family and to the success of the cotton industry established there by David Malcomson.

Industrial villages developed in Britain as a solution to the requirements of industrialists using waterpower for manufacturing and who needed to assemble and control a labour force in isolated rural areas. Advances in the development of steampower reduced the dependence on water and by the 1830s industry had acquired an urban environment. Later nineteenth-century industry driven village developments were schemes of building and improvement carried out by established businessmen who were anxious to improve the working and living environment of their employees. These included the development of Saltaire by Titus Salt, completed in 1871, Bournville developed by George Cadbury and the construction of Port Sunlight began in 1871 by W.H. Lever.[1] Bessbrook, county Armagh, was an early Irish example of this type of development conceived by John Grubb Richardson who in 1846 began the task of building a linen industry embracing a community which was to be a temperance colony without public house, pawn shop or policeman.[2] Close family connections between Portlaw and Bessbrook were established in 1867 when John Grubb Richardson's son James married Sophia, a daughter of William Malcomson. Curved felt-roofed houses similar to the Portlaw houses were built in James Street and Frederick Street, in Bessbrook. Bessbrook tradition has it that these roofs were incorporated in the village houses at Sophia's insistence, to remind her of Portlaw.[3]

Steam-powered industry was slower to develop in Ireland so that rural villages created to house large industrial populations were developed throughout the nineteenth century. Regionally, they were an Ulster phenomenon, concentrated spatially in Down and Armagh. The majority were built between 1830 and 1870, their development associated with advances in the mechanization of linen production (figure 2). The new mechanised mills needed to attract labour in large quantities and from the 1830s onwards many of the employers built villages to cater for their workers. These include Seapatrick, Sion Mills and, most interesting in the context of the present study, the village

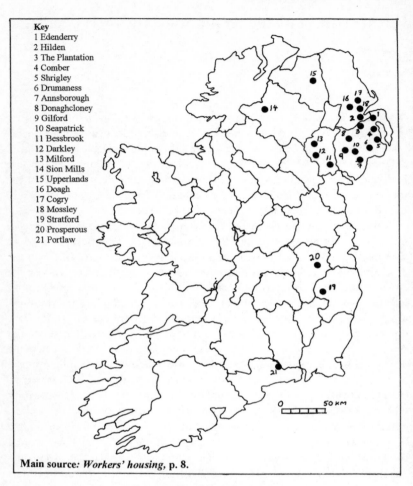

Key
1 Edenderry
2 Hilden
3 The Plantation
4 Comber
5 Shrigley
6 Drumaness
7 Annsborough
8 Donaghcloney
9 Gilford
10 Seapatrick
11 Bessbrook
12 Darkley
13 Milford
14 Sion Mills
15 Upperlands
16 Doagh
17 Cogry
18 Mossley
19 Stratford
20 Prosperous
21 Portlaw

Main source: *Workers' housing*, p. 8.

2. Industrial villages in Ireland, 1750–1900

of Dunbarton/Gilford where much of the social infrastructure put in place closely parallels similar developments in Portlaw.[4] Portlaw was a slightly earlier development than most of these villages and is distinguished from them also by the fact that the core area of the village was totally redesigned and remodelled in the early 1860s.

David Malcomson was the founding father of Portlaw. He was a Clonmel, county Tipperary, based flour miller and a member of the Society of Friends. He began his flour milling enterprise in partnership with Richard Sparrow c.1795[5] but by 1807, he was working independently having taken possession of the 'Corporation Mills'.[6] Over the next decade he became the dominant figure in a region that dominated the milling industry nationally. In 1822, he expanded his enterprises into county Waterford when he negotiated a fifty-three year lease on a mill at Pouldrew (near Kilmeaden), county Waterford, a short distance from Portlaw.[7] Malcomson became involved in flourmilling at a defining moment in the history of the business. The nature of the industry had changed from a small scale one, grinding small amounts of corn on a commission basis for local farmers, to a large capital intensive and in David Malcomson's case export-oriented one. The Malcomson business became one of the leading exporters of flour through the port of Waterford. In the period 1820–29, an average of 21 per cent of flour exported from Waterford was Malcomson's.[8]

David Malcomson's decision to expand his business empire to include the manufacture of cotton was apparently inspired by the visit of James Cropper, a fellow Quaker, to Ireland in November and December 1824. Cropper suggested that the problem of Irish poverty could be solved by establishing cotton manufacturing in Ireland.[9] Matters of a more immediate concern motivated David Malcomson into diversification. He feared that the corn laws were about to be repealed and the consequences of this action would be serious for his flourmilling and exporting business. These concerns were articulated in a letter of 18 April 1825 to Richard Ussher when he wrote

> we fear we are on the wave of such a change in the Corn Laws as will be very injurious to this country. Canadian wheat is to be admitted at a duty of 5s. per barrel and of course we apprehend a large quantity from the States will be smuggled in as such. Foreign wheat is likely to be admitted at a low duty. It is clear that for every barrel of foreign corn imported from foreign countries into England she wants so much less from Ireland.[10]

Six days earlier, two areas of Portlaw land forming 'a most eligible situation', were leased from John Thomas Medlycott and his son. The first area containing 4 acres 3 roods 17 perches was leased for a period of 999 years, at an annual rent of £15. The leased land was located at Mayfield on the site of a corn or flourmill and which had been completely destroyed by fire in 1818. The lease included access to all headweirs, millraces, mill ponds, watercourses and streams.[11] The cotton complex and its ancillary developments were constructed on this site.

A second area of land containing 'thirteen acres or thereabouts plantation measure', on which the Mayfield dwelling house was situated was leased for a period of thirty-one years or three named lives, at an annual rent of £50.[12] This area formed part of the site where David Malcomson was to construct the workers' cottages in what developed into the industrial village of Portlaw.

Prior to the arrival of David Malcomson this site had been the centre of a flour milling complex. Included on the site were the two flour mills of Mayfield mills, a large mill house and stores in which was contained two grist mills and bolting machinery, a range of offices including clerks offices, apartments and a bake house.[13] An iron mill was also situated adjoining the flourmills.[14] David Malcomson would almost certainly have examined this site and become aware of its waterpower potential when seeking to expand his milling business, before eventually settling on the Pouldrew complex. In settling for the Mayfield site he was following closely the advice of James Cropper as set out in his letter of December 1824 to James Pim of Dublin and published in the local press in January 1825. Here Cropper expressed a preference for

> taking a population to a waterfall, rather than bringing a steam engine to the people as it would be an advantage to separate the people who are to be employed, with a view to an improvement in their habits.[15]

A wide range of tasks had to be accomplished if the enterprise was to succeed. A factory building was required, plant, machinery and raw materials needed to be sourced and transported, a labour force had to be recruited, trained and provided with accommodation, considerable environmental manipulation was vital to ensure the essential water power and finally markets that would be continuous and sustainable needed to be identified.

David Malcomson was now embarking on what was to become his most spectacular business venture. At sixty years of age he had amassed the finance to cover the considerable fixed and working capital required to establish an enterprise of the scale imagined by Cropper. He had the experience of managing and shaping a labour force as well as working in the export market where his network of contacts and knowledge of ships and shipping would now be put to further use.

The original village of Portlaw encountered by David Malcomson in the early 1820s contained a cluster of about seventy cabins and was situated to the south of the River Clodiagh in the parish of Guilcagh. French traveller De Latocnaye, visited the village in 1796 and found accommodation in 'a miserable cabin, the horrible shelter of abjectest poverty', on the edge of the village and his account offers a valuable description of conditions there at the end of the eighteenth century. 'Half a dozen nearly naked children were lying on heaps of straw, pell-mell with a dog a cat, two hens, and a duck. Never in my life had I seen such a hideous spectacle'.[16] Admittedly unreliable census returns show that its population doubled between 1818 and 1831 (Table 1).

Table 1. Population of original Portlaw village (Guilcagh parish), 1818–31

	male	female	families	houses inhabited	uninhabited	building	total population
1818	292						
1821	195	200	80	71	1	0	395
1831	269	320	116	89	0	0	589

According to the Malcomson family memoir the lease of the site of the original village terminated in 1836 and the proprietor levelled about eighty houses forcing nearly all the families occupying them to cross the Clodiagh and take up residence in the industrial village.[17] This area retained the main

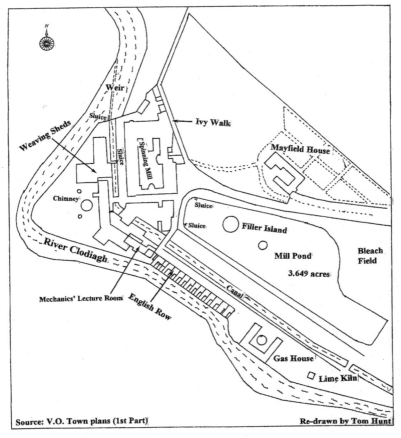

Source: V.O. Town plans (1st Part)   Re-drawn by Tom Hunt

3. Factory unit, Ivy Walk, English Row, and Green Island, 1850

public buildings of Portlaw, including in 1841, the Roman Catholic chapel, police barracks, dispensary, petty sessions house, a hotel and a public house as can be seen in figure 1.

David Malcomson faced the problem of attracting, controlling and maintaining a reliable and dependable workforce if the cotton manufacturing venture was to succeed. The provision of reasonable quality accommodation was essential to achieving this purpose. Factory construction was undoubtedly accompanied by a house building programme. The earliest housing developed was the three areas of English Row, Ivy Walk and Green Island constructed within the factory compound unit (Figure 3).

English Row, a terrace of fifteen slateroofed, stonebuilt houses, was built near the factory complex and locked between the river Clodiagh and the canal thus constricting its open space. These houses were in sound order and good repair in 1848. The terrace included a type of community hall, which functioned as a mechanics' lecture room, a reading room, a temperance lecture hall and a place of worship for Methodists.[18] Temperance advocate, John Finch who lectured there in 1836 described the hall as 'a neat and spacious building erected for the purpose, capable of holding six to seven hundred people, seated with forms'.[19] The houses were of a better quality than those of Green Island and were the residences of skilled personnel from the factory in 1848. Griffith's valuator identifies two land stewards, two millwrights, a carpenter, a wood-turner and a cashkeeper amongst the residents.[20] The last four houses in the row were shared between families each having a separate yard but having only one entrance. Each house had a small yard, in the words of the valuator, 'nicely enclosed by a wall and all in nice clean situation as private houses but I doubt as to it being wholesome being so low and near the factory'.[21] Ivy Walk, the second area of housing within the unit, was a collection of six superior quality houses located on the edge of the factory premises (Figure 3) and included Mayfield house which was a Malcomson family residence.[22] This was one of the finest houses in the county valued at £54 in 1850 (Figure 4).[23] The remainder of the Ivy Walk houses ranged in value from £1 to £9. These were described as being 'clean and comfortable for private use but not being very wholesome adjoining the factory'. Included in the area were the watchman's house and the factory dispensary which was located in part of a triangular shaped house, 'the under part of which is very badly lighted as the street in front of the house is raised to about half the height of the first storey'.[24] Green Island, was the largest of the areas and the last of the three to have been developed. A 999 year lease of the plot containing 4 acres 38 perches at a yearly rent of £10 7s. 3d. was negotiated from Thomas Curtis in September 1834.[25] Malcomson's building is unlikely to have commenced prior to that date. The earliest available map, that of the Portlaw boundary survey, carried out in September 1839, shows the Green Island development unfinished. The map

4. Mayfield house (late nineteenth century view), redesigned c. 1855 by John Skipton Mulvaney

was compiled to establish territorial boundaries so other aspects were less accurately shown, nevertheless the Green Island housing scheme is clearly incomplete as is the northern section of Mulgrave Street. The completed scheme formed an L-shaped development of fifty-seven houses, on the banks of the river Clodiagh, with frontage facing a green area of almost four acres (Figure 5). These were stone built, slated dwelling houses finished with lime mortar. Numbers 1–39 measured 13 feet in height and width with length varying from 11–14 feet. Numbers 40–57 were larger houses, each occupied by two families. These houses shared a uniform frontage of 14 feet, were 27 feet in length and 14 foot 6 inches in height. Each house in the street was enclosed by a small yard at the end of which was a privy.[26]

This area of factory and housing formed a distinctive plan unit, scarcely visible from the upper sections of the town and defined by its physical characteristics. Located at the base of a steep incline, it was separated from the rest of the town by the mill pond, bounded on the south and west by the Clodiagh river and overlooked from its elevated site to the north by the stately presence of Mayfield house and gardens.

Market Square (Figure 5) was located at the factory entrance. This was a U shaped terrace of thirty-two slated houses, the majority valued at £2. 5s.[27]

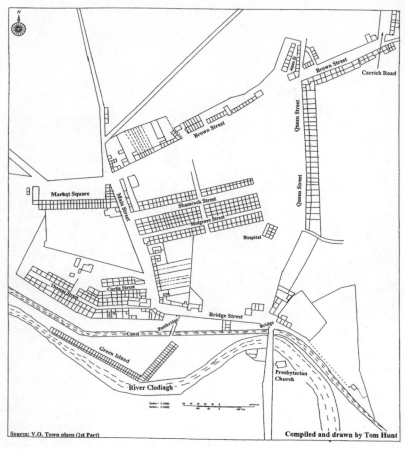

5. Portlaw 1850

Factory expansion increased the demand for housing and the Malcomson firm responded by building four parallel terraces, map evidence suggesting that the development was completed between 1840–1 with the building of the northern terrace of Shamrock Street (Figure 5). These were Shamrock Street with forty-six houses and Mulgrave Street with forty-seven, uniformly valued at £1 16s. in 1850. These thatched houses had an enclosed yard and had mud plastered stone walls. They were extremely small, sharing a street frontage of 20 feet, 24 feet in length and they varied in height between 6 feet 6 inches and 7 feet.[28]

The eastern edge of the town was defined by the thirty-three houses forming Queen Street. This terrace was completed between 1841 and 1845, the thirty-three houses recorded in the printed valuation 1850, were built by

December 1845 when the valuator carried out his original survey. The street was mainly a Malcomson one but here Joseph Malcomson (chief partner 1838–58) was a facilitator of housing development rather than a direct creator as in the other areas. Small parcels of ground were leased on which the occupiers built their own houses. The majority of residents were listed as paying an extremely cheap ground rent of only six pence per foot. At the time of building only a short time remained on the lease which reduced its value as development ground. The low ground rent attracted the attention of the valuator who compared its cost to Thomas Street and Curtis Street where 'the ground rent was 2 shillings per foot and in a far worse situation. The lease makes the difference'.[29] All houses were regularly inspected and kept in repair by the factory firm. Rents included a monthly supply of soap valued at 1 shilling. This was a characteristic feature of all their rentals, as the Malcomson social policy embraced the encouragement of personal cleanliness.

Monthly rents for the various Malcomson houses payable in 1848 are illustrated in table 2. In practically all cases the valuator commented that rents were reasonable which might be expected as the primary purpose was to attract workers to the area.

Table 2 Monthly rent and valuation Malcomson houses in 1850

Street	Valuation	Monthly rent in shillings
English Row	£3 5 0	varied
Green Island: 1–39	£2 6 0	6
Green Island: 40–57	£2 18 0	5
Market Square	£2 4 0	6
Mulgrave Street	£1 16 0	5
Shamrock Street	£1 16 0	5

Source: V.O. house books. Primary valuation of tenements

Developments at Portlaw provided opportunities for individuals with capital to invest in housing to profit from the Malcomson requirements and expansion. Thomas Curtis was an entrepreneur who took advantage of the demand for housing created by the development of the cotton industry and he speculated by constructing a separate unit of housing, offering direct access to the factory compound. Curtis had married the widow of James Daniel, a miller and one of the previous lessees of the site held by David Malcomson.[30] Fifty-four houses in total were constructed, eighteen in Curtis Street and forty-six in Thomas Street (Figure 5). By 1848 these thatched stone walled houses were 'deteriorated by age, and not in perfect repair', and were considered to be 'in a backward bad, dirty unwholesome situation and yet were let at a very high rent'.[31] The northern edge of the town was defined by Brown Street, on land the property of the Medlycott estate and by 1850 contained seventy-four housing units, 50 per cent belonging to the Rev. John Thomas Medlycott. Malcomson Brothers at this stage had an interest in only six houses in Brown Street.

The Medlycott family arrived in the area in May 1775 when the lands at Mayfield, consisting of 40 acres, were leased from Edward May by Thomas Medlycott, 'formerly of the city of Dublin, but being seized and possessed of large estates in Ireland including Killowan in the county of Waterford,' for the sum of '£7,000 of the currency of Ireland', and a yearly rent of £500 'of like currency'. The lease also included 176 acres of land at Rocketscastle and 200 acres of land at Gurtardagh and Coolroe (where Malcomsons developed their cotton factory). By 1790 these lands had been purchased for the consideration of two £5,000 payments.[32] As a landlord Medlycott was the facilitator of all the Portlaw developments as he was prepared to grant all the required leases.

Despite the high quality of much of the housing in the town it did not escape the growth of a suburban cabin sprawl, a common and widely commented on feature of the morphology of towns in nineteenth-century Ireland. A northern extension of Brown Street, the Carrick Road, was lined with mainly mud-walled thatched cabins, sixty-one on the west side in the Coolroe townland and fifty-eight in Mayfield.[33] These were developed by Medlycott and four of his tenants. An 1839 report described them as 'a long line of miserable huts', that were 'a disgrace to the town'. 'They appeared to harbor a great deal of destitution' and the residents persisted with 'the shameful habit of rearing manure heaps outside the door'.[34] In 1848, fifteen houses on the road, the property of Dr James Martin, true to his moral values and anxious to encourage self-improvement amongst the labourers, had been 'put nicely in repair' and had their rents reduced from £3.15s. annually to 5s. monthly.[35]

In 1850 the town consisted of a central core of four parallel streets enclosed by Brown Street to the north, Queen Street to the east and Bridge Street to the south. These areas were separated by large areas of open space which provided ample possibilities for future expansion or redevelopment (Figure 5). West of this area, and practically hidden from view lay the factory compound including the residential areas already described. The town consisted of twenty-four streets, a wide open thoroughfare leading to the factory and 625 dwellings[36] catering for a population of 4,351.[37] An examination of the age and building quality index used by the Griffith valuation surveyor in Portlaw,[38] establishes Curtis Street and Thomas Street as the areas of poorest quality housing within the town.

Contemporaries visiting the town were impressed. These included Mr and Mrs Hall who visited in 1842 and felt

> that the town and neighbourhood of Portlaw have of course shared the prosperity of the Malcomsons. The houses are clean and comfortable, the people are all decently dressed; there is an air of improvement in everything that pertains to them.[39]

Less than six miles away Carrick-on-Suir presented a dismal appearance to Henry Inglis when he visited in 1834. He was

> struck with its deserted fallen off appearance, with the number of houses and shops shut up, and windows broken, and with the very poor, ragged population that lingered about the streets. I had not visited any town in a poorer condition than this.[40]

Factory inspector James Stewart, experienced in urban conditions, was extremely impressed by the state of developments at Portlaw. In his 1842 report he commented that

> Portlaw in Ireland afforded far better and more comfortable accommodation than, so far as I have observed, is to be found for any other of the working populations in any other parts of Scotland and Ireland.[41]

Despite the impression made on contemporary visitors the Malcomson firm decided in the late 1850s to substantially remodel the core element of the town. The formality of the new Malcomson development was inspired by the baroque planning ideas that characterised the great European seventeenth and eighteenth-century cities. Essential features of this style including the regular wide streets, uniform house frontages and straight axes terminating in a wide open market place were replicated at Portlaw in a minature scale.

The Portlaw town plan departed from the essentials of this style by the total exclusion of 'architectural set pieces' such as churches or courthouses.[42] The final version displayed the three criteria, identified by Graham and Proudfoot, as the most powerful discriminators of formality, namely the spatial ordering of the building plots, the regularity of the street plan and the presence of a geometrically ordered marketplace.[43] The radical change in the morphology is illustrated in figure 6 which shows the 1870 town plan superimposed on the 1850 version of the town.

This physical transformation was confined to the Malcomson part of the town and was motivated by a variety of social and economic factors. It was partly inspired by a desire to alleviate overcrowding which certainly would have troubled the Quaker social conscience. Following the demographic upheavals of the famine the town's population increased by 19 per cent (Table 3). Movement from the rural portion of the Clonagam parish to the town had caused severe overcrowding in 1851 with 245 families squashed into 137 second class houses and 638 families occupying 364 third class houses.[44]

Table 3 Population changes in parish of Clonagam, 1841–51

Clonagam population: 1841–51	1841	1851
Rural portion	1112	684
Portlaw town	3,647	4,351

Source: Census of Ireland 1841, p. 248; 1851, p. .356.

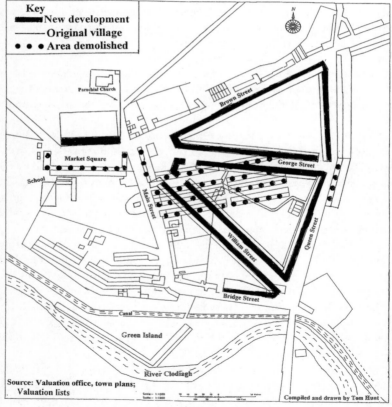

6. Morphology change: new development superimposed on original design.

The valuation report of 1848 considered Mulgrave and Shamrock Streets to be slightly decayed. Fourteen years later they are likely to have deteriorated further and to have been seriously overcrowded so that the time had come for their replacement.

Legal formalities for the new development were completed in 1852 when the area of land of the original three life lease was purchased from Thomas Medlycott for the consideration of £1,500.[45]

William Malcomson, was the chief partner of the firm when much of this radical intervention in the townscape took place. The development gave practical expression to his views on the beneficial effects of proper management and care of a landlord's tenantry, outlined in his address to the members of the Portlaw Agricultural Society at their annual show in October 1862. He suggested

> the more they identified the labourer with the locality in which he was, the more they identified him with the success and interests of the farm or estate on which he worked. He believed there was no field in which so little had been done and so much remained to.be accomplished, as providing the agricultural labouring class with good and comfortable dwellings. He did not think the proper kindness and countenance was shown to the labourer that he deserved. [46]

Treating employees properly brought immense benefits to the employer as 'the Irish labourer was a grateful recipient of the slightest favour'. Apart from the practical consequences from such actions, people of property had also a moral responsibility to care for their tenants.

> It was not for blessings or success they should always look, they should remember that they were only doing their duty to their neighbour, their country, and their God, and they would feel a satisfaction in their own minds, whether their exertions were appreciated or not, that would compensate them for their efforts.[47]

The period of reconstruction coincided with a period of tremendous economic success for the Malcomson family business. Expansion and diversification was taking place in several different enterprises and geographic areas embracing linen milling at Belfast, an integrated linen complex at Carrick-on-Suir, land reclamation at Tramore and the purchase of a salmon fishery at Lax Weir in Limerick.[48] Confidence was high and building developments at Portlaw were a visible expression of this confidence. The development of new housing stock also represented a sound economic investment offering the prospect of a rapid return on the costs. Tenants and rents were guaranteed provided the Portlaw enterprise remained viable.

Malcomson's pride in their business achievements and confidence in the future found visible expression in the alteration or construction of at least seven mansions for various family members, to the design of the architect John Skipton Mulvaney. This association with Mulvaney began with the aggrandisement of Mayfield House c.1855 for Joseph Malcomson. Following his death, his sons built mansions of their own including, in Portlaw the magnificent neo-classically styled Woodlock for Frederick Malcomson and the less grandiose Clodiagh Cottage for George Pim Malcomson.[49] These prestige symbols were a vivid landscape expression of the status of the Malcomson family and delivered a clear message as to the leadership of local society.

New development of the town began with the construction of a terrace of fifty two-storey houses on the south side of Brown Street, work which was completed by 1859.[50] Redesign of the town required the demolition of Mulgrave Street, Shamrock Street and the northern part of Main Street. The open space thus created was infilled by two triangular areas of housing the apex of each pointing to an enlarged and redesigned Market Square. A third partly completed triangular area was formed by William Street and the eastern half of Bridge Street. The regular plot sizes and streetscape of the completed streets and the contrast with the remainder of Bridge Street and Main Street is clear evidence that the plan devised for the town remained unfinished.

Such was the pace of development taking place in Portlaw in the early 1860s that the valuator recommended that 'in sending out the books for revision it would be as well to leave some blank pages as they will be required in consequence of all the additional houses in Portlaw'.[51] Mulgrave and Shamrock Street were demolished by 1862. Ten houses were constructed on the south side of George's Street and up to forty houses in William Street. By 1867 sixty-three houses were occupied in the latter street and fifty-five in the former. Substantial changes were also carried out in Queen Street. Twelve houses of uniform value were completed by January 1858 on its western side, 'although no gardens as yet were struck out for any of them', and by February 1867 this had been extended southwards by the addition of a further thirty houses, bringing the total number of houses in the street to seventy-five.[52]

Mansion building and the enclosure of private Malcomson demesnes impacted on the development of the streetscape of the town and in particular George Pim Malcomson's work on developing his demesne to the east of the town. Seventeen houses at the eastern extension of the southern side of Brown Street had been demolished by February 1864 and their sites 'let in with Mr. Malcomson's demesne'. Constructing the demesne wall also involved some remodelling of the eastern side of Queen Street. This was carried out in 1867 when the first twelve houses forming the southern extremity of the street were removed.[53]

Other areas of the town also experienced change. The original houses of Market Square were all taken down by March 1867 and their sites enclosed by

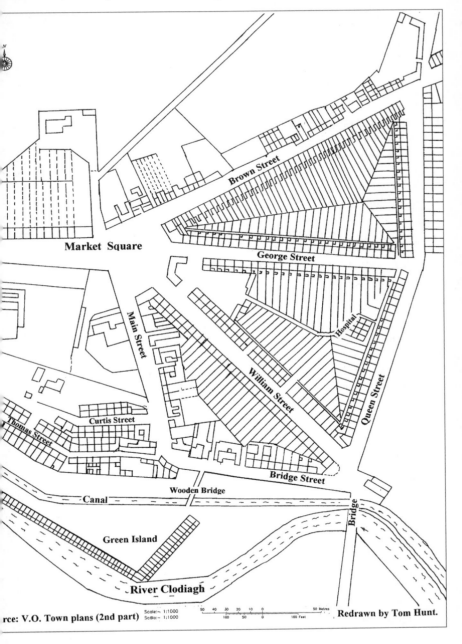

Market Square

Brown Street

George Street

Main Street

Hospital

William Street

Queen Street

Curtis Street

Thomas Street

Bridge Street

Bridge

Canal

Wooden Bridge

Green Island

River Clodiagh

rce: V.O. Town plans (2nd part)

Scale:- 1:1000
Scale:- 1:1000

50 40 30 20 10 0   50 Metres

100   50   0   100 Feet

Redrawn by Tom Hunt.

7. Portlaw 1870, unitary planned central core

a stone wall and planted. Two years later ten small slated cottages, valued at £2 each, were completed on the northern edge of the square by landlord Thomas Medlycott. The use of English Row as a residential area was discontinued; the houses were now used as stores and according to the valuation officer in March 1868, 'will not again be set to weekly tenants'. Numbers 8 and 9 were converted into an added facility for the workers with the installation of Turkish baths. The northern section of Browne Street also underwent redevelopment but of a much more piecemeal nature that included the housing infill of certain areas and the enlargement and improvement of several residences.

The quality of the Malcomson housing developed in this phase was far superior to the original and is reflected in the assessed valuation. The two-storey Malcomson houses in Browne Street were valued at £5 annually; the new single storey houses of Queen Street, William Street and George Street, at £3. The old Mulgrave and Shamrock Street houses they replaced shared a uniform valuation of £1 16s. each in 1850, reduced to £1 10s. by the mid 1860s.[54] The quality and construction standards used is emphasised by the fact that many of these houses are still inhabited and structurally sound at the present time.

House-construction followed a uniform pattern. The outside walls were stone built and rendered with a lime plaster; the dividing walls were built of brick. Bedroom floors were boarded and those of the kitchen and passages asphalted.[55] Each room had a fireplace and chimney and each kitchen included a range, with an oven and side tank with tap for hot water. Practicality was essential in the planning of these houses for the fireplace and chimney were located on the end walls of each house allowing back to back fireplaces. The rooms had twelve foot high ceilings, which gave a great sense of space and airiness.

Architecturally, the most distinctive feature of these houses were the special roofs developed by the Malcomson firm. Curved trellised softwood frames formed the roof trusses. Short lathes were then nailed to the base of these frames to form the house ceiling. Lathes, held in place by flat topped nails, covered the curved section. The framework was then covered with several layers of tarred calico. The tar was a by-product of the firm's gas works located within the cotton factory compound. The frames were constructed to provide substantial overhanging eaves at the front and back of the houses. Both trellised frames and covering material were manufactured at the factory. Consequently this method of roofing was less than half the cost of conventional slate roofs. The tarred canvas cost 9s. per yard, three quarters wide, but became more expensive in the early 1860s, increasing to a shilling a yard, 'owing to the advance in the value of the material'.[56] The single storey dwelling houses cost £40 to construct,[57] with the total Malcomson investment in housing estimated at £10,000 in 1871.[58] The Browne Street two storey houses contained a parlour and bedroom on the ground floor and back kitchen. Two bedrooms were located upstairs. Each house had an enclosed paved back yard and a small garden. The rent charged for these houses was 10 shillings per month. Single storey terraces were developed in the two newly created streets, William Street and George Street as well as in Bridge Street and Queen Street. These houses were three roomed with a front parlour and had a kitchen fitted with ranges and ovens. The majority had enclosed back gardens. Monthly rent charged was 8 shillings.[59]

The completion of the Malcomson building programme saw the emergence of a two-tiered urban landscape in Portlaw. Newly built Malcomson areas were enclosed by areas that had experienced little change. Changes in the northern section of Brown Street were confined to infilling of certain sections and some general improvements. Thomas Street and Curtis Street were unchanged as was most of Main Street. This aspect of the town's development attracted the attention of one of the country's leading surgeons in the mid 1860s. The town was described by Doctor Mapother as a mixture of the 'healthy and prosperous' with the 'sickly and ruinous'. Malcomsons' owned 332 houses which were clean and comfortable and in which preventable diseases were one fourth less frequent than in the remaining 278 'squalid houses' of the town.[60]

8. Wide, straight, George's street, flanked by small terraced houses and leading into broad Market square (c.1900).

The growth of the industrial village began with the establishment of the factory in 1825 and continued to 1850, when the first phase of town development may be considered completed. Other proprietors were also prepared to invest in housing to meet the demands of the labourers who were arriving in the town on a continuing basis. The next phase of development, 1855–65, saw the original townscape radically altered, the planned morphology emphasised by the uniform house design, wide streets and regular shaped garden plots. Economic circumstances prevented the completion of the third triangular area. In Portlaw the grandiose formality of the streetscape was tempered somewhat by the architectural simplicity of the modest housing that defined the essence of each street (Figure 8).

The social world of the village

The Malcomson development at Portlaw did not confine itself to simply developing an adequate physical infrastructure that would prove sufficient to attract and maintain in reasonable conditions of comfort a reliable workforce. From the beginning, members of the Malcomson family or some of the key factory personnel were involved in the establishment of a number of social institutions aimed at encouraging personal development and adding an interesting and healthy social environment to a congenial working one.

The Malcomson-owned Mayfield stores, stocked clothes and groceries at reasonable rates and catered for basic shopping needs. The use of tokens[1] (2s. tokens were introduced in 1834, 1s. in 1838 and 4d. tokens in 1839) to pay the operatives presented opportunities for exploitation as had happened at English mills operating the truck system. This was not the case in Portlaw where participation was optional and where the store in six years trading to 31 July 1841 reported profit margins of 4 per cent, returning a profit of £866 on a turnover of £20,925.[2] A joint stock company, with close factory associations,[3] operated a bakery.[4] Others also took advantage of the commercial opportunities presented by a large industrial workforce in receipt of a regular income. Main Street was the main retail street with the shops strategically placed to take advantage of the operatives emerging from the factory premises. This street contained fourteen hucksters' shops, four groceries and a joint stock bakery in 1848.[5] Despite the emphasis on temperance, public houses were an important part of the social and economic life of the town. The numbers employed in the factory required that workers from each department had a different pay day,[6] so that all days were likely to have been shopping days in the village.

Health and welfare in the early days of the community were catered for by the dispensary but in January 1835, to ensure that workers were healthy and remained so, a resident surgeon, Dr James Martin, was appointed to the factory receiving an annual salary of £100, 'with apartments'.[7] Concern for workers' welfare and a desire for the speedy return of absent staff to the workplace motivated factory management to place a list of those absent from work before Dr Martin every morning so that all cases of illness or of injury resulting from accidents were attended to within a short time after they occurred. The factory inspector complemented the success of the Malcomson firm in dealing with health issues in his report of 1842. In the period 1835–7 Dr Martin kept an accurate 'bill of mortality' and he found that deaths in the

688 persons then employed in the factory amounted to only twenty while the mortality rate amongst the 270 outdoor staff amounted to sixty-nine.[8] A fever hospital of four terraced houses, located in Queen Street, which was also under the supervision of Dr Martin, was supported jointly by the Malcomson firm and workers'contrributions.

Workers who became ill and were unable to continue at work were catered by the Mayfield Provident Society which administered a system of social insurance. Persons under fifty years of age considered by the committee to be 'well conducted and healthy', were eligible for membership. Others became eligible for membership by paying double the usual monthly rate but their widows or children were excluded from death benefits. Illness benefits ranging from 16 shillings to 2 shillings per week was paid for the first four months of sickness on payment of a 'corresponding number of halfpence'. After four months benefits payable were halved.[9] The rates of benefit equated to approximately half an operative's weekly wage. Widows or 'such of his children or his nearest relations', of a deceased member were entitled to an allowance of six weeks wages to be paid at times the officers considered 'most to their benefit'.[10]

The society was paternalistic as the rules required that the members subscribed to a set of regulations that restricted their social behaviour. A member bringing 'illness or accident on himself by drunkenness, debauchery, rioting, quarreling, or playing at unlawful games on the Sabbath' was ineligible for benefit. A member in receipt of benefit discovered to be 'acting imprudently, or in a manner likely to retard his recovery', was likely to have his benefit reduced by half.[11]

Temperance was a concern for the management and in the 1830s the value of temperance was vigorously promoted at the Portlaw factory. Operatives that lived a sober lifestyle would be healthier and more efficient workers. The early emphasis at Portlaw was part of a wider national concern to encourage temperance and reflected the strong tradition of temperance activity within the Quaker community. The first large-scale societies appeared in Ireland late in 1829, with Belfast and Dublin being the main centres of the movement, although the first society established was the New Ross temperance society, in August 1829 at a Society of Friends' meeting house. The medical profession also played an influential role in the early Dublin temperance movement.[12] Factory doctor, James Martin, a fellow of the Royal College of Surgeons in Ireland and a certified practitioner in midwifery from the south-eastern lying in hospital South-Cumberland Street, Dublin[13] was likely to have been influenced by his Dublin experience and throughout his time in Portlaw was a strong advocate of temperance.

Temperance devotees used a variety of methods to deliver their message. Advocates appreciated the need to entertain as well as to instruct their audiences and soften their harsh message. This was a tactic used in Portlaw. Itinerant preachers styling themselves 'kings of reformed drunkards', were used for this purpose.[14] Thomas Swindelhurst, 'king of the reformed drunkards' of Preston, visited the factory in the summer of 1836 and in December, John Finch, a Liverpool iron merchant, 'spoke about two hours, challenged all opposers', before declaring himself 'king of the teetotallers'. He claimed twenty-four new converts to teetotalism bringing the factory total to eighty-seven and if moderate drinkers were included, 500 in total were pledged to temperance.[15]

On 24 March 1838, the Portlaw Tontine Club, was established to 'promote temperance and the habits of saving'.[16] The rules of the society were carefully formulated so that a member in breach of the rules was penalised financially, and this formed an effective controlling device for the society. Shareholders paid sixpence weekly and at the end of a twelve month period (later reduced to six months) the entire capital with interest was divided amongst the members. However any member convicted of being intoxicated or of giving or taking drink in a public house within four miles of his own residence was expelled from the society without recompense. To ensure sobriety after the payment of the yearly dividends a member was required to leave 5 shillings on deposit which was paid within a week provided no charge of intemperance was substantiated against the member.[17] Substantial sums were available for paying dividends. The *Waterford Chronicle* reported that in March 1839, £239 was divided amongst the members and in October £267.[18] These figures would suggest a membership of approximately 400. The same issue emphasised the pressure to conform operatives who had difficulty with the concept of temperance were placed under, as well as the tolerance factory management was prepared to exhibit. It was reported that factory manager Robert Shaw, after unsuccessfully trying every other means' had sent a dozen of the factory operatives, 'for whom the fascination of the Rosy God had proved too powerful', to Cork for the purpose of 'their visiting the great moral reformer, the very Rev. Mr. Mathew'.[19]

The impact of the movement impressed factory inspector James Stewart, who reported in 1841 that 'every vestige of intemperance had now disappeared in Waterford'.[20] Portlaw was specifically identified the following year, where 'the workers adhere rigidly to the Temperance system of Father Mathew, and would not, on any terms, associate with persons of dissipated habits'.[21] The promotion of temperance remained an abiding concern, throughout the period of this study whether encouraged indirectly by societies such as the Mayfield Literary Society or directly by the temperance societies.

Education was one of the key social institutions encouraged by nineteenth-century paternalistic employers. The concern of the Malcomson family for schooling was partly motivated by enlightened self-interest, partly by religious faith and partly by the requirements of factory legislation. The result was the development at Portlaw, from the 1850s, of a set of educational institutions that were unparalleled within the county.

According to the family memoir, David Malcomson regretted his own limited education and his lack of opportunity of learning the history and occurrences of past ages.[22] His commitment to education is evident from his last will and testament in which he made substantial bequests of £100 to the Provincial Schools of Waterford and Lisburn, £50 to a similar school at Mountmellick and £200 to the Brookfield Agricultural school at Ballinderry, county Antrim.[23] When the Portlaw factory was established in 1826, the existing legislation[24] required that apprentices and others be instructed 'in the usual hours of work in reading, writing and arithmetic' to be 'provided and paid by the master' in 'some room or place in such mill or factory to be set apart for such purpose'.[25]

David's son, William, chief partner in the company from 1858 to 1876 had clear ideas of the economic value of education. He believed that nothing could be more requisite 'in the developing the production of the country' than the introduction of education.

> The man who can both work and think was able to produce more in any employment than the uneducated worker. If they had not an educated class of labourers they could not get a fair day's work from the machinery.

This was the message he delivered to the members of the Iverk Agricultural society in October 1876.[26]

From the beginning a school was established inside the factory grounds. In 1827 the children of the factory were instructed in reading, writing and the elements of arithmetic. No interference with their religion was attempted.[27] Official information is available on the Malcomson input to education in the 1830s. The commissioners of public instruction reported in 1835 that the Malcomson firm, since 1833, subscribed £13 annually for the maintenance of a day school, funded a school house, provided a teacher's residence and supplied fuel to the school. The school was attended by sixty males and twenty females paying 1*d.* weekly.[28] A night school was also maintained. Jonathan Binns, an expert on Irish social conditions following his work as one of the assistant commissioners for the 1830s Poor Inquiry, paid a visit to the day school in 1836. Accompanied by Dr Martin, he was impressed by

> the extreme quickness of the Irish children; little creatures of seven years old pointed out the different countries on the maps and their

peculiarities stating the distinctive productions of each; and the older boys read and wrote in a superior manner and were well versed in mathematics.[29]

Information is lacking on educational develoments in the 1840s. Maguire reported the presence of an infant school and one for more grown girls in the early 1850s under the 'care of and supported by Mrs Malcomson' in which everything 'like sectarian interference with the religious tenets of the children is sedulously avoided'.[30]

The Malcomson contribution to education was increased substantially in the 1850s. Work, which was in progress in 1845,[31] on an impressive school building, bearing many of the stylistic features of the architect J.S.Mulvaney, was completed. The building of stone and lime with a felt roof was furnished to a high standard. The male room contained fifteen desks with forms attached capable of accommodating 150 pupils as well as a teacher's desk and several book presses. The female section included twelve desks and attached forms suitable for use by 200 pupils. The rooms were reported as being large, bright and well ventilated, measuring seventy feet in length, thirty in height and twenty feet in width, with boarded floors and plastered walls.[32] Each room was lighted by six windows opened by pulleys.[33] Total construction costs were £2,000 and the firm estimated in 1868 that their annual contribution to education amounted to £200. In this U.K. wide survey by the factory inspectors only five firms reported spending more on a school structure.[34]

Within this imposing complex separate male, female, evening and infant schools were organised, each affiliated to the national board of education. The Mayfield female school was established in February 1855[35] and affiliated to the national board in June. Grant aid, in the form of a £25 salary for the teacher, Mary Jane McAllister, and books for the use of one hundred students was awarded. Number increases justified the award of an assistant's salary in October 1855. Education was secular, concentrating on reading, writing, arithmetic and the elements of history and geography.[36] The curriculum was extended in November 1858 when Margaret McNamee was employed exclusively for the teaching of needlework. Instruction in plain and ornamental needlework, knitting, netting, crochet, cutting out and embroidery was given for two hours each day.[37] The performance of the principal teacher Mary Jane McAllister was singled out for particular attention in 1859. She was awarded a supplemental or good service salary of £5 per annum as a reward for the 'zeal, faithfulness and efficiency exhibited by her in the discharge of her duties'.[38] However, her assistant was the subject of a number of unsatisfactory reports by the inspectors before she was finally dismissed in October 1875. Vocal music was included in 1862 and was so successful that the girls 'sang some pieces from Moore's melodies with commendable taste', on the occasion of the visit of the lord lieutenant, Lord Wodehouse, to the factory in November 1865.[39] In the 1870s the firm was experiencing trading difficulties and these are reflected in the performance of the school. In September 1874 the manager was requested to see that first class pupils were more systematically taught and that sufficient attention be paid to the teaching of grammar and geography. The following month attention was called to the lack of order and discipline in the classes. Despite these relatively rare expressions of reservations the firm continued to provide a worthwhile education for the female population of Portlaw. The opening of the Portlaw convent school in July 1883 provided an alternative for the girls of the town and numbers attending the Malcomson school declined rapidly. Average attendance declined from seventy-three in June 1883 to fourteen in March of 1884. In October 1884 management closed the school as there was no prospect of numbers increasing.[40]

The male school was established on 2 May 1855 and affiliated on 22 June with similar grant aid to the female school,[41] and continued to provide education for the boys of Portlaw into the twentieth century. The curriculum was similar to the female one with vocal music also introduced in 1862. The reports for the period of study were generally satisfactory with the complaints of the inspectors mainly concerned with routine administrative matters.[42]

The Mayfield infant school was established in September 1859. Children paid 1*d*. per week with some being admitted free at the discretion of the manager. Hours of attendance were from 10 am to 3 pm during the week and from 10 am till 12 noon on Saturday.[43] Infant schools were popular institutions in working class districts as they provided cheap reliable sources of child care for working mothers. They also provided an antidote to the problem of the early removal of children from school to workplace and provided a basic education for children at a very early stage.[44] The attractiveness of the infant school is reflected in the relatively high numbers of children enrolled. Reliable attendance figures are available for the period 1859–73 and it wasn't until 1871 that the number of pupils enrolled at the female school surpassed the number of infants. Attendance was however extremely poor ranging from a low of 25 per cent to a high of 37 per cent.

Evening schools were characteristic social institutions advocated and provided by benevolent reformers anxious to encourage self improvement and self help.[45] A male evening school was established in Portlaw in July 1855 and remained open throughout the school year. Classes were conducted from 7.30 pm to 9.30 pm during the summer months and from 7.00 pm to 9.00 pm in winter. The students, paying 1*d*. or 2*d*. weekly, were the 'mechanics, cotton spinners, weavers, carders and those engaged in various other occupations connected with the Portlaw factory', who in the opinion of the inspector seemed to be 'most desirous to improve their literary condition'.[46] This school provided an opportunity for learning for operatives who had not received adequate education during the day, as they were employed in the factory. The

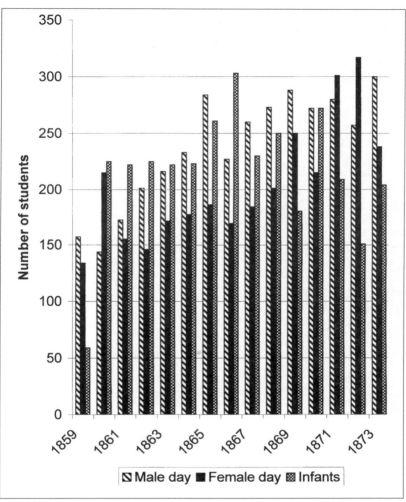

9. Number enrolled, Mayfield day schools, 1859–73
Source: Appendices to *Reports of commissioners of national education*, 1859–73, pp. 126, 128, 134, 136, 220, 144, 172, 470, 493, 337, 552, 558, 505, 557, 530 respectively.

curriculum was exclusively secular concentrating on spelling, reading, arithmetic, geography, grammar and history.[47] An evening school for the female factory operatives was established at the same time.

The annual reports of the commissioners of national education provide statistical information on the performance of these schools, including enrollment and attendance figures as well as measuring the students' proficiency based on the level of lesson book in use. The reports are

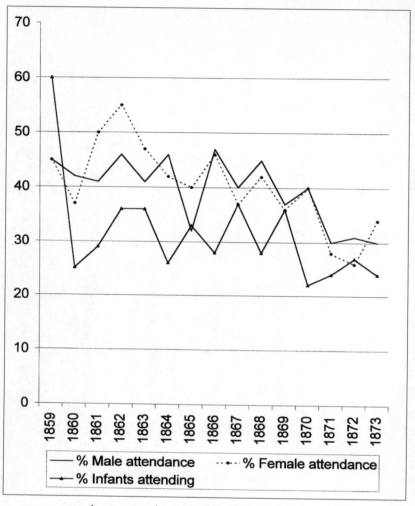

10. Average attendance at Mayfield day schools, 1859–73.
Source: Appendices to *Reports of commissioners of national education*, 1859–73, pp. 126, 128, 134, 136, 220, 144, 172, 470, 493, 337, 552, 558, 505, 557, 530 respectively.

particularly detailed on the period 1859–65, including information on the level of book studied by the pupils. Information on enrollment and average attendance for the infants' school and female and male day school is summarised in figures 9 and 10.

The Powis Commission reported in 1870 on the performance of the Irish national education system and identified a number of serious problems. Less than one third of the children on the registers were in average daily

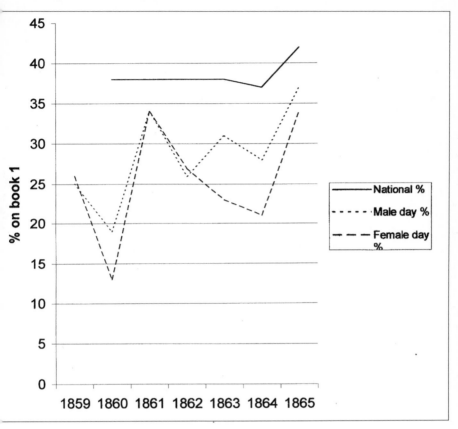

11. Proportion of students following book 1 nationally and Mayfield, 1859-65.
Source: Appendices to *Reports of commissioners of national education, 1859-65*, pp. 126,
128, 134, 136, 220, 144, 172, respectively; Powis, i, pt. 1. p.290.

attendance.[48] This was attributed to parental indifference.[49] Attendance was
largely a matter of parental discretion and parents who sent a child to school
faced the double burden of school fees and sacrificing a child's earnings.[50]
Children rarely progressed beyond third class. In Waterford county only 4 per
cent of students and nationally only 7 per cent were above third class. Poor
attendance and early leaving impacted on literacy levels. The Powis commissioners found that in 1867, 45 per cent of the pupils were at the first book
level, 32 per cent at the second level and only 7 per cent in the fourth book
which was considered extremely low. Students did not achieve full literacy
until the sequel class (following the second book) where they were expected
to read 'with a fair degree of ease and correctness,' and to write on paper.[51]

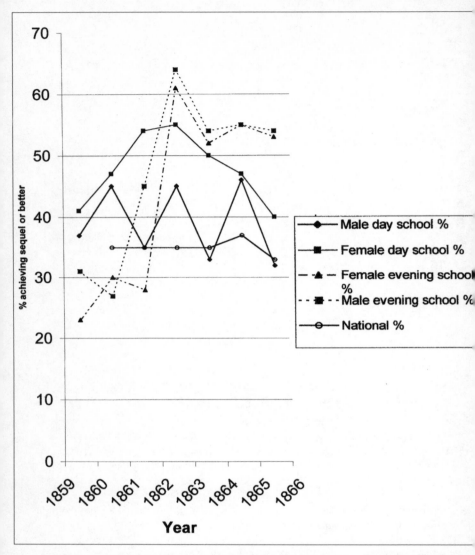

12. Proportion of students achieving sequel level or better nationally and at Mayfield, 1859–65. Source: Appendices to *Reports of commissioners of national education*, 1859–65, pp. 126, 128, 134, 136, 220, 144, 172, respectively; Powis, i pt. 1. p. 290.

The Portlaw average attendance at both male and female school (40 per cent) was similar to the national average, for the period 1859–73 and tended to fluctuate from year to year, declining in particular from 1870 (Figure 10). Attendance for some children in the town became compulsory after 1862 when the firm began employing children under fourteen in the factory. These were the half-timers, who formed *c.*8 per cent of the workforce in the period 1867–74 and were required by factory law to attend school on a part time basis. These attended school free of charge, the firm contributing two pence per week towards their education.[52]

The performance of the Malcomson Portlaw schools differed from the national trend in a number of instances. The male school achieved superior standards with an average of 29 per cent of students at book one level (Figure 11) and 38 per cent progressing to the sequel level or higher. The female day school achieved even better standards with 48 per cent of the students at the sequel level or better (Figure 12). This was related to the presence of the infants' school as many of the children entering the primary system would have basic literacy and consequently spent less time on book 1.

Standards of literacy were slightly higher in the evening schools with the proportion of children achieving sequel level or better greater than in the primary schools between 1861 and 1868 and far better than the national trend. Average attendance displayed much the same pattern as the day schools with the female students the better attenders. Attending evening school after a day's work was difficult as was the task of concentrating on the school work[53] and required a high degree of motivation.

The impact of the schools was reflected in changes in literacy rates in the town. Census data provides information on literacy levels in the town for the period of study. In Portlaw town and county Waterford levels were particularly low. In 1841, 71 per cent of the county population could neither read or write; only two counties had higher levels of illiteracy.[54] Of the 140 towns ranked by the commissioners who compiled the 1841 census, the town of Portlaw had the fifth highest percentage (58 per cent) of illiteracy in the country.[55] Despite the best efforts of the Malcomson firm, matters had disimproved by 1851. The great famine had caused severe population displacement, in-migration swelling the town's population from 3,647 in 1841 to a peak of 4,351 in 1851,[56] and increasing the number of illiterates in the town by 6 per cent (Table 4).

Table 4   Per cent changes in standards of literacy, Portlaw, 1841–1871

	1841		1851		1861		1871	
	Male	Female	Male	Female	Male	Female	Male	Female
Literate	13	7	14	8	13	12	18	18
Read only	10	13	5	9	6	8	6	9
Illiterate	22	36	24	40	24	37	19	30

Source: Census reports: 1841, p. 249; 1851, p. 357; 1861, p. 257; 1871, p. 973.

The new system had made some impact by 1861 with an improvement of 3 per cent in the overall levels of literacy; females were the chief beneficiaries their levels of literacy improving by 4 per cent. The level of illiteracy was still extremely high at 61 per cent. In 1871 the impact of the Malcomson system can clearly be seen. Illiteracy was reduced to 49 per cent; 36 per cent of the population now considered themselves able to read and write. Females of the town were the greatest benificieries as female literacy improved by 10 per cent between 1851 and 1861.

Other less formal methods of encouraging male education were in place. From the beginning a news and reading room was included in the factory complex. It contained a variety of English and Irish newspapers including *Blackwood's*, the *New Monthly Magazine, Kaleidoscope, Dublin Literary Gazette, Farmer's Journal* and 'fifty small volumes which were the gift of David Malcomson'. This was organised by the Mayfield Club with the intention of destroying ignorance and vice by producing virtue, temperance and intelligence among the working classes.[57]

More definite information is available on developments in the 1860s. The Mayfield Literary Society was established in 1859. Malcomson Brothers were the patrons of this society and supported a heated gas-lighted reading room. Individual family members made financial donations and contributed literary material.[58] The society's 1863 income of £29.14s. included contributions of £23 by Malcomson family members.[59]

A variety of intellectually challenging and entertaining activities were organised by the society. These included debates between members and with societies of a similar nature,[60] lectures, musical evenings, literary reading sessions and spelling competitions.[61] The members also had access to a library (containing 780 volumes in 1871[62]) and reading room where the society supplied a wide range of national and international newspapers. These are illustrated in table 5 (Malcomson supplied papers in bold).

Table 5 Newspapers available in reading room 1864

The Freeman's Journal	*Cassell's Paper*	*London Journal*
Illustrated London News	*The Irish Times*	*The Practical Mechanics'*
The General Advertiser		*Journal*
The Times	**The Waterford Mail**	**The Munster Express**
The Telegraphic Circular	**The Bombay Standard**	

Source: Waterford Mail, 24 April 1864.

Judged by the published annual reports, the Portlaw society was an active one. In 1862 thirty-four meetings were held; fifteen devoted to debates, thirteen for readings and six lecture sessions.[63] The following year thirty-nine meetings were held of which twenty-two were devoted to debates, thirteen to lectures or essays and four to readings. Topics of debate included political, philosophical and topical issues as can be seen from the 1863 programme illustrated in table 6.[64] Chosen themes established an agenda of issues which the officers felt a well-educated young person should contemplate and discuss intelligently.

The addresses, delivered by various gentlemen associated with the society at their annual soirees, illustrate the philosophies, values and moral standards which it was hoped would be inculcated from membership. These acknowledeged the value of hard work, sobriety, temperance and encouraged sabbatarianism. These were typical of the attitudes associated with the evangelical Protestant revival of mid nineteenth-century Ulster.[65]

William Malcomson stressed the importance and value of debate for both participants and listeners. The latter had 'their thoughts brought into action, and their minds considerably enlarged'. As their 'minds became enlarged their prejudices were dissipated, and they were led to see the great dependence of every member of the human family on each other'.[66] Participants compared their ideas on the different subjects, one person receives instruction from another, and in this way realised 'how dependent each person is on another'.[67] This belief in a community of common interest was a key element of William Malcomson's social philosophy and one which he put into practical effect with social and infrastructural improvements carried out during his time as the main partner of the company. In his 1869 address to the society other values were emphasised. The necessity to do well whatever task was undertaken was 'the great secret of success in life'. Listeners were advised to 'show their respect to their Maker by attending at their place of worship on the Sabbath and endeavouring to spend that day of rest well'.

Reading was an essential ingredient in the recipe for success in life. Success was not possible 'without an unswerving course of reading, not spasmodic and desultory attempts at reading, but steady persistent study'.[68]

Typically, for the medical officer Dr Martin, 'the elevated pleasures' of the society offered a superior alternative to 'wasting the hours at the corners of the streets, indulging filthy jests and hateful slang.' Reading the pages of 'contemporaneous history,' as presented in the daily press was far better than spending time 'within the sphere of the brutalizing influence of strong drink'.[69]

Associated with the literary society was the Mayfield Philharmonic Society. This small society, established in 1864, specialised in performing 'negro melodies'.[70] The programme of songs performed at one of the early concerts is illustrated in table 7.

Table 6 Topics of debate Mayfield Literary Society, 1863

Was the impeachment of Warren Hastings a just act?

Would universal suffrage benefit the nation?

Is the theatre an institution that ought to be encouraged by the state?

Does the political career of the duke of Wellington entitle him to the gratitude of British subjects?

Which has conferred greater benefits on mankind the pen or the sword?

Was government justified in sending a special commission to Tipperary in 1862?

Would foreign intervention in the American struggle be justified?

Will the present age be as illustrious in history as that of Elizabeth?

Is it desirable to retain the hereditary character of the House of Peers?

Whether it would be for the good of the country that the present system of land tenure should be altered?

Is there danger in over educating the people?

Is emigration beneficial to Ireland?

Whether the Negro race is benefited by being slaves in America or left in its original state?

Ought England to interfere on behalf of the Poles?

Should principles give way to expediency under any circumstances?

Whether was Fox or Fitt superior as orator, statesman or politician?

Should capital punishment be abolished?

Should not the fiscal business of countries be taken out of the hands of the grand jury and be vested in a jury composed of ratepayers, elected by open voting from each barony annually?

Is not the system of flogging in the army, navy and in schools a violation of natural rights, contrary to all principles of religion, humanity and sound policy?

Was the bombardment of Kagosimis, by an English fleet, under Admiral Kuper, justifiable?

Is a stipendiary or unpaid magistracy the better for the administration of justice?

Source: Waterford Mail, 27 April 1864.

Societies such as these encouraged education informally and were also an attempt to create alternative social outlets to the pubs and drinking houses by providing an opportunity for social intercourse and recreational diversion, through tea drinking, reading rooms and participation in bands, dances and processions. Newspaper accounts of the *soirees* of the Mayfield Literary Society describe meetings organised to a formula that was almost ritualistic. Meetings

Table 7 Performance programme of Mayfield Philharmonic Society 1865

Mayfield Philharmonic Society
Programme of performance: February 1865.

Sing, darkies sing	Lily of the valley	De ole kitchen
Walk, chalk, ginger blue	Beneath the weeping willow	Ladies, wont you marry
Flora Bell	Julianna Brown	Louisianna Bell
De ole grey goose	The hour for thee and mee	Erin my country
Sally come up	Up squash and downe de middle	Dandy Jim
Going home to Dixey		

Source:Waterford Mail, 17 February 1865.

began with music played by the band of the society, followed by partaking 'of the cup which cheers, but not inebriates', accompanied by 'sweet bread, cakes, oranges, jellies and other delicacies'. [71]

Malcomson Brothers, in common with several English Quaker firms such as the Crosfields of Warrington, Cadbury's of Bournville and Huntley and Palmer of Reading[72] devised ways of showing their appreciation for the work done by their employees. The factory supper was one such way. It was normally held during Christmas week, with the clerks and heads of departments of the various concerns of the firm in Clonmel, Waterford, Portlaw and Carrick-on-Suir assembled in Portlaw for the 'annual entertainment', held in the school rooms.[73] The factory workers were treated to a similar night of entertainment. Annual outings were also organised for the Portlaw operatives and were reported in contemporary newspapers. In 1863, a special train ferried three hundred employees to Killaloe for the annual outing.[74] In July 1865, 'a fete of truly magnificient scale,' was given by Robert Malcomson at his demesne at Kilcommon, Caher, county Tipperary, to 'about 280 of the Mayfield factory hands and the heads of the various departments at Portlaw and at the Neptune shipbuilding foundry at Waterford'.[75] The assemblage must have represented a curious spectacle to the inhabitants of Caher as they marched through the town accompanied by their own band making their way to the 'principal gate at Kilcommon demesne'.[76] A ship launch at Maclomsons' Neptune shipyard was an occasion of great carnival

and excitement in Waterford city. The Portlaw employees frequently attended
these launches as part of a company outing and treat. The occasion of the
launch of the *Magnet* was typical. The employees were granted a special
holiday on the occasion and were brought by train to Waterford city to witness
the launch. Following the launch, 'the excursionists numbering approximately
eight-hundred' were taken on a sea cruise, circling the Saltee islands, aboard
the river steamers *Ida* and *Tintern*.[77] These outings offered the employees a
welcome relief from the monotony of the mill routine. They acted as bonding
agents between operatives, management and proprietors, established a sense of
community consciousness and encouraged the notion of communal
enterprise.

   Malcomson family special events were also occasions of great celebration
and festivity in the town. The marriage of Sarah Sophia Malcomson to James
Richardson, 'representing a union between the two greatest of Irish
commercial firms', was one such occasion.[78] The *Waterford Mail* captures some
sense of the atmosphere, colour and excitement in the town as the couple
returned from the marriage ceremony in Waterford city. 'Thousands' collected
in William Street to witness the bridal procession, the street presenting

> a peculiarly animated appearance, the houses being all dressed up with
> evergreen and mottoes, and two large triumphal arches studded with
> flags and bannerets being erected across it at each entrance. Flags also
> floated from the Mayfield shop.[79]

Spectators flocked to the bride's house at Milfort and 'the cheering was again
heartily repeated'.

> The Mayfield band then played a well selected programme after which
> the vast crowd dispersed. Cannon were discharged at intervals during
> the day, and in the evening a very effective display of fireworks were set
> off.[80]

The scene at the entrance to the factory at Mayfield was equally impressive,
where a 'large gas jet was suspended over the front gate; it bore the word
"Welcome," with the initials J & S., the heraldic device of the Malcomsons
forming an ornamental centre piece'.[81]

   William Malcomson remained faithful to his concept of society as an
organic community in which the constituent groups were dependent on each
other and benefitted by their mutual co-operation when he organised the
post-marriage reception. The main banquet at Mayfield house included a
guest list that would do justice to the marriage of a merchant prince's
daughter. The attendance included three M.P.s and some of the most

prominent Quaker business-men of the time. However refreshments were also 'liberally supplied' at the newly built gymnasium. Here, 'the three dancing rooms afforded accommodation for about 500 people, comprising principally the operatives of Mayfield'.[82]

Physical recreation and team sport became part of the social curriculum of the town in 1864, when the Mayfield cricket club was established and played its first match against the Fiddown club on 15 August.[83] The secretary of the club was William Dunkerley, who was probably its founder and who seems to have had some experience of the game. In a 1869 game against Fiddown he returned fifty-two runs before 'carrying out his bat'.[84] A gymnasium was also opened in the Market Square in 1867.[85]

The range of paternalistic social provision made available to the residents of Portlaw carried the essential stamp of Quaker benevolence which distinguished much of their nineteenth-century economic enterprises throughout Britain.[86] The primary motivation for these developments was economic. Temperance and health care improved worker efficiency; education produced operatives that were more capable of managing machinery and equipment. Membership of the welfare societies was tightly controlled and restrictive of personal behaviour. Membership of the Provident Society was confined to those who were 'well conducted', benefits were paid to widows at a time that was considered to be 'most to their benefit'. Festive and social outings encouraged the idea of a community enterprise.

In Portlaw the Quaker influence was enriched considerably by the zeal of factory doctor James Martin who wielded considerable influence in the town. He fulfilled one of the key roles required of many Quaker business employees; the more senior the employee the more active he was expected to be within the wider community.[87] He was a tireless champion of the idea of self improvement and was of the tradition of the mid-nineteenth century evangelical Protestant reformer.[88] A founding member of the Portlaw Agricultural Society[89] and its long term secretary; a temperance zealot and an ever present speaker or officer at Mayfield Literary Society soirees, his influence in the creation of the town's social policy and provision of social institutions was substantial.

The world of the factory: physical structure, power, plant and equipment

Manufacturing cotton cloth involved three distinct procedures, spinning the raw cotton into yarn, weaving the yarn into cloth and the completion of various finishing processes such as dyeing and bleaching. These usually took place in different establishments. At Portlaw, the Malcomson enterprise progressed during the nineteenth century to become fully integrated encompassing all three distinct processes, a development that was the exception rather than the rule. An elaborate support structure was also established at the plant designed to make the complex as self-sufficient as possible. This chapter examines the structure of the factory complex, the internal organisation of the manufacturing processes, the use of power resources and the variations over the period in the use of spinning and weaving machinery.

Having taken possession of the site, David Malcomson began the construction work almost immediately. In July 1825 it was reported that over one-hundred masons and labourers were employed at the site. Construction involved considerable capital expenditure. The main water wheel was cast at Cork at a cost of £1,000.[1] In 1828 David Malcomson estimated that £60,000 had been spent on construction[2] and by 1846 an additional £40,000 had been expended.[3]

The spinning mill was constructed in two stages. The southern section was initially constructed and a northern extension was later added. The mill was fully completed by 1836. The dimensions of 260 feet in length and 40 feet in breadth as given by Samuel Lewis in 1837 were those of the completed spinning mill.[4]

The overall form was typical of early nineteenth-century English mills. It was a six storey rectangular building, tall and narrow in proportion to its length.[5] Adequate internal natural lighting was an important factor in the mill design so windows occupied a large proportion of the wall space (Figure 13). Typical windows were vertical rectangular shaped, glazed with thirty small panes of glass in each. The south gable featured a full-height stair tower giving access to all floors of the building. Different construction techniques were used on both parts of the building. The southern part was timber floored made from beams of imported memel pine supported by cast iron hollow columns. The floors in the north portion were constructed of brick arches resting into

13. The Mayfield spinning mill, Portlaw, county Waterford.

saddle backed cast iron beams supported by hollow cast iron columns. This created a strong fire-proof section with iron doors installed on each floor to act as fire guards.[6] This fire proofing technique was of the most modern design similar to contemporary English developments.[7]

The single storey weaving shed, with characteristic saw-toothed roof, was constructed to the west of the canal (Figure 3). The glazed sections of the roof faced north and were angled steeply to prevent sunlight shining directly into the shed, an important matter in weaving coloured cloth.[8] Later extensions to this section were also necessary as the loom numbers increased significantly in the late 1850s and early 1860s.

An elaborate water system, which required heavy construction work was developed to serve the needs of the factory. The mill pond, (3.6 acres in extent) was the key to this system (Figure 3). This pond was fed by a culvert which ran underground from the sluice on the Clodiagh river at the north end of the factory. From the south-west end of the pond a second culvert fed water on to a wheel which provided power to drive the pumping plant. The water for the mill operations was drawn from the Filler Island which was connected to the pumping plant by a 10 inch cast iron pipe. It was then pumped to a small pond (0.5 acre) situated in the grounds of Milford House, the residence of William Malcomson. From here the water fell by gravitation to supply the needs of the entire factory and fire hydrants.[9]

The Portlaw cotton plant was powered by steam and water. Initially David Malcomson was impressed by the waterpower potential of the site but steam engines were introduced soon after the factory was established, Malcomsons

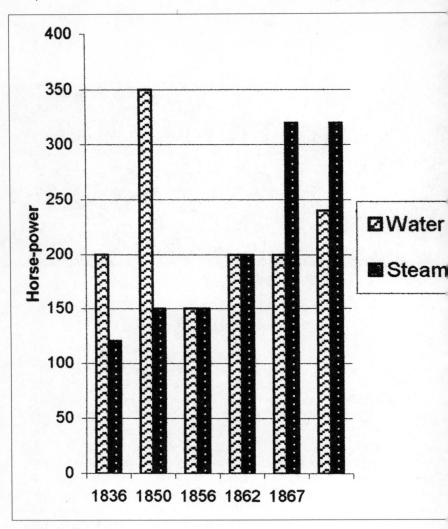

14. The changing relationship between water and steam power in Portlaw, 1836–70. *Source: R.I.F.,* 1836, pp 348–9; 1850, p. 10; 1857, p. 16; 1862, p. 19; 1868, p. 23; 1871, p. 71.

'not having obtained facilities for making a dam'.[10] The changing relationship between water and steam power in use in Portlaw between 1835 and 1870 is illustrated in figure 14. Over the period under review, the importance of waterpower declined. In 1870 steam supplied 60 per cent of the power used, a reversal of the 1835 position. In 1835 waterpower to the value of 200 horse power was produced at Portlaw. Two massive overshot wheels provided 160 horse power and a smaller wheel 40. David Gaffney carried out detailed measurements of these wheels in December 1845 for the Griffith valuation, and their dimensions are re-produced in table 8. By this stage the Portlaw plant with three engines capable of generating 120 horse power, had developed considerable steam potential. This was essential as the water supply from the Clodiagh was inconsistent; steady for six months from October to March, at half supply during the months of August, September and April and at quarter supply for May, June and July. During the 1860s steam power became more important. The steam capacity increased from 200 to 320 horse power between 1862[11] and 1867.[12] There was greater need for the regularity of steam power as production increased and machinery and equipment became more sophisticated. Linen mules were installed which were heavier and less suited to water power. Tow (coarse flax fibres) was spun and this made heavy power demands requiring one horse power to work forty spindles whereas up to 1,000 mule spindles handling the finer cotton fibres could be driven by a similar power supply.[13]

Table 8 Dimensions of water wheels in use at Portlaw in 1845

	Wheel one	Wheel two	Wheel three
Diameter	34'	26'	22'
Breadth	16'6"	15'0"	8'6"
Buckets	84	60	48
Depth of shrouding	17"	18"	16"
Revolutions per minute	2.3	3	3.2

Source: V.O., Field survey book, p. 1.

David Malcomson embraced both the worlds of flour and cotton in his business career and in the internal organisation of the processing of the raw cotton, Malcomson or his engineer, Robert Shaw, adapted for the cotton mill at Portlaw some of the organisational methodologies used in the Malcomson Clonmel flour mills. The late-eighteenth century flour mills stored the grain on the top floor and the various processes were then carried on in the intermediate and ground floors. The system introduced in Portlaw for the spinning of raw cotton into yarn is broadly similar to the one used in flour milling and was very different to that used in Lancashire cotton mills. In these mills the ground floor was normally used for storage, a feature that became more common as the century progressed. Preparation and carding took place on the second floor and the spinning mules were located on the upper storeys.[14] In Portlaw the raw cotton was raised to the top floor and the various processes were carried out in the intermediate floors with the spinning carried out on the lower floors.

The task of converting raw cotton into yarn involved three main processes, embracing a wide range of tasks and skills. Newspaper reporters visited the Portlaw complex in the 1850s[15] and 1870s[16] and provided detailed and graphic descriptions on how these processes were organised. The first stage involved the opening and initial preparation of the bales of raw cotton. They were carried from Waterford by barge up the river Suir and then via the river Clodiagh and canal directly into the basement of a storehouse. The canal linked the factory and the Clodiagh and was built to by-pass a shallow section of the latter river. The canal also functioned as a mill race and tail race. On arrival the bundles were ripped apart by a machine called 'the devil'. This machine had strong, sharp, rapidly revolving teeth that tore apart the lumps of cotton. Willowing and scutching then took place. Willowing machinery consisted of a large drum filled with iron spikes. These loosened and separated the fibres and a powerful fan blew away impurities through a large pipe. The scutcher removed further impurities from the willowed cotton by beating it with rapidly revolving metal blades. The raw cotton was then blown by fan to the top of the factory building and the various processes began on the top in a system that was the reversal of the English one. The cotton was then thrown on to a slowly-moving cloth, beaten and subjected to a strong current of air which blew off any remaining dust.

The second stage of the process involved carding and the production of roving, a thick cord of cotton fibres. On the completion of this process the loose cotton was transformed into a ribbon approximately one and a half inches wide. The roving frame was then used to combine six or eight of these into one band. The cotton in an untwisted state at this stage was then moved downstairs where the third stage took place when the roving was stretched and twisted on the spinning machines to produce the yarn. In the 1870s two modes of spinning were in use at Portlaw – mule spinning and throstle spinning. The latter produced a fine strong yarn that was cheaper to spin than on the mule. Some sense of the atmosphere that prevailed in the spinning sections was captured by the 1876 reporter

> By far the most sensational spectacle of the place is the throstle spinning room, with its wondrous maze of machinery in which the young operatives are immersed like victims cast into the toils of some huge many limbed monster, only that the faces have no expressions of pain upon them and the ceaseless whirr and rattle mingles not with any human cry. More interesting though less exciting is the mule spinning. The machinery looks simpler and does its work with an almost silent calmness that gives one the idea of its being possessed of intelligence.[17]

Several of the storeys were devoted to these operations and on completion of the spinning the yarn was unwound from the bobbins and wound into hanks prior to weaving. The ground floor of the main building was chiefly devoted to the dyeing process. The yarn was then carried to the weaving sheds where at one stage over nine-hundred power looms were employed in the manufacture of cloth. The woven cloth was checked for quality and this was followed by the measuring process which was 'accomplished by a machine which lays the cloth over an arc equal to the standard unit of length'.[18]

The final stages of production involved completing the various finishing processes. The calendar process, 'akin to ironing', was one of the most noteworthy. The piece of cloth was brought on a beam or wooden cylinder and fixed on the front of a large machine composed of a series of cylinders. The centre cylinder was heated by steam, those above and below were wooden and tightly covered with paper. The cloth, unrolled in a damp state from the beam, was passed round the heated cylinder and pressed against it by the other cylinders with a pressure equal to many hundred weights. This process was designed to give the cloth a proper finish.[19] Smaller pieces of cloth were subjected to the bittling process. Rolled upon wooden cylinders the pieces of cloth were beaten by a series of vertical staves until they acquired a 'beautiful gloss'.[20] Finally the cloths were sent to the dispatch rooms where they were folded on the long tables and sent to the dispatch loft and made up into bales, 'compressed into the smallest possible compass by powerful hydraulic presses, wrapped in canvas and bound with iron hoops, for the long voyages, and duly branded and labelled for exportation to the ends of the earth'.[21]

The Portlaw development included an ancillary range of buildings forming an impressive industrial complex in their own right. These included

> a large foundry and workshops in which every implement and appliance required in the mill is specially manufactured. Everything in the way of machinery and fitting, from the huge 20ft. iron mill wheel to the tiny wooden bobbin, is produced here for the establishment, and such is the wear and tear of a huge mill like this that the whole series of workshops and their staffs of mechanics are kept in constant employment.[22]

The pattern room stored thousands of molded wooden patterns used in casting the various machine parts that were required in the mills or weaving shed. The workshops included a saw mill, a turners' shop, the pattern makers' shop, the painters' and glaziers' shops and the harness makers' quarters, 'where the driving bands, great and small, for the machinery are made and the iron spindles receive their buffing with leather before they are ready for the mill.'[23]

Contemporary reports establish between eighty and one-hundred skilled craftsmen in regular employment in these sectors. This was not an unique feature of early cotton mills, particularly in isolated areas. New Lanark for instance operated a machine shop that cost £8,000 annually to run and employed almost one-hundred men.[24]

The factory inspectors returns, after 1850, provide reliable information on the use of spindles and powerlooms in the factory (Table 9).

Table 9 Spindles and powerlooms in use in Portlaw 1850–74

Year	1850	1856	1862	1867	1870	1874
Spindles	26,055	27,000	30,292	43,253	41,792	41,908
Powerlooms	626	900	940	844	837	812

Source: R.I.F., 1850, p. 10; 1857, p. 16; 1862, p. 19; 1868, p. 23; 1871, p. 71; 1875, p. 7.

The returns identify a number of important features of the development of the industry at Portlaw. The powerloom weaving section expanded rapidly during the 1850s. 339 power looms were reported in use in the firm in 1835;[25] and their numbers had increased only to 360 by 1839.[26] Over the next eleven years weaving expanded slowly; 266 additional looms were added. The section expanded spectacularly between 1850 and 1856 when the number of powerlooms installed increased by 44 per cent from 626[27] to 900.[28] This dramatic growth pre-dated a similar increase in Great Britain, where the increase was 20 per cent over the same period. British expansion was greatest between 1856–62 when an increase of 34 per cent took place.[29] This difference is easily explained as many of the British firms were still using handloom weavers. There was no tradition of handloom weaving in Portlaw. There was however a link between the Portlaw factory and the Malcomson handloom weaving plant in Clonmel. This seems to have been established to cater for the yarn that was being produced at Portlaw but the firm faced problems in attracting and maintaining a labour force at Clonmel. Both Robert and David Malcomson complain about the high rates of absenteeism amongst the operatives and their lack of 'constancy' at work.[30]

Powerloom weaving created heavy labour demands and the additional looms in use in Portlaw significantly increased the workforce. It required fivefold as many operatives in proportion to the capital invested as did spinning, 'being as labour intensive an industry as spinning was capital intensive'.[31] The labour required was essentially the unskilled labour of machine minders and was normally provided by females and adolescents. Thirty-two additional adolescent males, 158 females and ninety-six adult males were added to the Portlaw staff between 1850 and 1856.[32] The extra powerlooms would have required the hiring of an additional female staff of up to 150 operatives to tend the looms. The normal ratio in the Portlaw weaving sheds was one female operative for every two powerlooms. In addition ancillary male labourers would be required for the preparation of the cotton, as overseers in the weaving sheds and in the finishing departments.

The period 1850–56 witnessed only a small change of 4 per cent in the number of spindles employed in Portlaw.[33] In 1862, the number of spindles had increased by 12 per cent to 30,292[34] and increased again by 43 per cent to 43,253 by 1867.[35] This dramatic increase in spindles however may not have generated significant extra employment. Throughout this period the spinning mule was becoming more sophisticated and faster in operation. In the 1830s 350–400 spindles per mule was the norm, by the 1850s 500 had become the average number; this rose to 750–900 by 1875 and by 1876, 1,000 spindles per mule had become the usual.[36]

The disused milling site that David Malcomson took possession of in 1825 was within a short period converted to an industrial complex that was without parallel in Ireland in terms of its scale and employment generated. The creation involved considerable environmental manipulation to supply the essential water and water power supplies as well as the cheap water transport that was essential in ferrying the raw cotton and finished yarn and cloth to and from Waterford. The technically sophisticated complex adopted some of the methods used in contemporary flour mills and applied them to the spinning process giving this section of the business an internal organisation very different to that used in Britain.

Comparison with contemporary British cotton firms underlines the scale of the enterprise that developed at Portlaw during the nineteenth century. Gaskell has outlined the essentially pyramidal hierarchy of firms that characterised the Lancashire industry in the early 1840s. Large firms were still few at this time and 'small to middling (and single-process) firms were predominant'. Of 321 Lancashire firms engaged in spinning and weaving only twenty-two employed a labour force of over 1,000 operatives.[37] At the end of the 1830s therefore the Portlaw factory was equal in status to firms at the apex of the Lancashire pyramid. In 1862 the average Lancashire firm employed 159 operatives at a time when Portlaw had 1,412 employees.

At this stage the Malcomson family presided over possibly the largest Quaker industrial concern world wide, employing as they did over 1,600 workers at the Portlaw plant in 1867.

The world of the factory:
personnel and markets

The integrated complex developed at Portlaw was labour intensive providing a wide range of opportunities for both skilled and unskilled male and female operatives working in a variety of conditions. The viability of the enterprise depended on the identification of reliable and continuous markets. This chapter investigates working conditions, labour rates and variations in the workforce and its structure concentrating on the period 1836–74. Markets and products are also examined concluding with a brief look at some of the reasons for the final collapse of the business.

Working conditions, the nature of the work and the age and gender of the workforce varied between the mill departments. Men dominated jobs requiring physical strength including the preliminary cleaning and sorting of the raw cotton, the preparation of the cloth for dyeing and printing, storing, hauling, loading and unloading the cotton and stoking boilers. In English mills this was poorly paid, low status work carried out in an unhealthy environment. Strippers and grinders who were responsible for cleaning and maintaining the carding machines had to endure an unpleasant dusty environment. Such workers generally suffered from high incidences of tuberculosis, bronchitis, asthma and byssinosis. Much of the work in bleaching and dyeing was also hazardous, involving exposure to strong poisonous chemicals.[1]

Powerloom weaving was essentially womens' work in the cotton industry and such was also the case in Portlaw. Visitors presented this work as light and relatively unskilled involving nothing more difficult than 'supplying fresh shuttles as the old ones are exhausted of their thread and of mending the thread in case it becomes broken'.[2] Noise was the chief environmental hazard that the labourers had to contend with in this area. In the words of a contemporary reporter, 'the clatter is something awful,' but the writer displayed extraordinary foresight when commenting that 'the young people, boys and girls, who spend their working hours in the midst of it, suffer no detriment from the noise.'[3] Womens' subordinate role within the workforce was emphasised in the weaving shed. Reporters described male 'overlookers' moving about the machinery. It was 'their business to see that the machines are doing their work right, and that the girls are attentive to it'.[4] The ratio of female weaver to male overseer in this department at Portlaw was normally twelve to one.[5] This characteristic of the weaving shed reflected patterns of gender relations characteristic of the partriarchal family with men occupying the managerial and supervisory positions.[6]

The culture of working long hours for low pay was an established part of contemporary economic practice. It was also an essential feature of Quaker business management. Robert Malcomson in his evidence to the handloom commissioners described the working hours during the 1830s at the Malcomsons' Clonmel handloom weaving plant. In the winter months the hours of work were from seven in the morning until eight in the evening with forty-five minutes allowed for breakfast at nine o'clock and an hour for dinner at two o'clock. Summer working hours were from six in the morning until seven in the evening.[7] Similar hours are likely to have been worked in Portlaw. In the mid 1840s the factory was working a sixty-nine hour week accumulated by working an eleven and a half hour day (excluding an hour and a half for breakfast and dinner). In the course of the year the workers enjoyed eight half days free from work with Christmas day and Good Friday closed days.[8] Special company outings and organised festivities were also part of Malcomson company culture and were organised at regular intervals and were described in the previous chapter.

Textile industries had their hours of work controlled by legislation with factories subjected to regular inspection to ensure that the legislation was operative. The act of 1847 limited the work of children, young persons, and women to ten hours but in practice it influenced the working hours of all factory employees. This act was introduced in two stages culminating in the introduction of a ten hours working day or fifty-eight hour working week from 1 May 1848. Such were the importance of the specified categories of worker to the industry in general that adult male workers were equally restricted, and the overall effect of the act of 1847 was to reduce the length of the working week for all operatives.

This act created serious difficulties for large industrial concerns and was the subject of much controversy at the time. Messrs. Malcomson reacted to this legislation by introducing the relay system to their work practices, and by increasing their workforce. Instead of working long shifts, sets of restricted workers were employed in separate short shifts during the day. The accumulated shifts reached the permissible total hours of work but this system was in breach of the spirit of the act as the workers were required to be in attendance in or near the factory for a longer period of time than the legislators intended. Factory inspector, James Stewart, reported in 1849 that the Malcomson firm were one of three in Ireland using the relay system and his report (by way of approval) included correspondence from the firm dealing with the matter. Malcomsons reported that 758 of the firms 1,240 employees were working by relays between 5.30 a.m. and 6.30 p.m. when 'all work ceases'. The system necessitated the hiring of 135 additional workers, at an estimated annual cost of an extra £4,000 in wages.[9] All relay workers had their names and their hours of work listed and posted in their departments and notice of their 'ingress and egress regularly posted at the entrance'. An overseer was especially employed to see 'that their ingress and egress are according to rule'.[10]

Every effort was made by the Malcomson management to create a working environment that was as tolerable as possible for the firm's operatives. Such were the efforts that the firm was singled out for special mention by the factory inspectors on a number of occasions. The apartments of the factory 'were large and well ventilated, and their temperature carefully regulated, by having the dust in the carding-rooms removed by a revolving fan'.[11] In his September 1843 report James Stewart was critical of ventilation standards in Irish factories but he excluded the Malcomsons' 'admirably conducted factory' from his criticisms. All the windows were 'so constructed as to open from the tops' and he was not sensible of any difference between the atmosphere in the apartments of the factory and in the countinghouse'. Fire escapes had been erected 'for the security of the persons employed by them on the exterior walls of that part of the factory which was first built.[12]

Despite the precautions danger was ever-present and the risk of accidents was constant. A contemporary newspaper described one such accident in graphic detail. Francis Shelly was an overseer in one of the spinning rooms who was unfortunate enough to allow his loose shirt become entangled in a revolving wheel, and the man was 'whirled into the machinery'.

> In a moment his two legs were cut off below the knees, and his body otherwise severly mangled. His body after a while got detached from the shaft and he was flung with great force through a window carrying the sash with him. He fell upon a platform outside, and when the other employees in the factory ran to his assistance he was dead.[13]

Factory discipline was strict from the beginning. According to Sheil, 'the strictest morality was preserved and it was the rule to dismiss any girl who was guilty of the slightest impropriety'.[14] A fining system was operated for less serious breaches of factory regulations. This was justified as being a more humane system than dismissing an operative from employment and the fines were paid into a factory poor-box.[15] The uncompromising attitude to serious breaches of factory discipline and the tensions emerging within the factory were evident in 1871 when a number of operatives refused to continue work and were charged with breaches of the Masters and Servants Act of 1867.[16] At a court hearing they were found guilty and fined.

The absence of detailed company records makes any examination of wage rates difficult. Apart from indicating that factory manager Robert Shaw was in receipt of an annual salary of £100, the surviving records of the 1830s make no mention of wages.[17] Factory doctor James Martin was similarly remunerated.[18] Therefore in considering rates of pay and in examining contemporary wage estimates it is important to bear in mind that two key members of the factory personnel were receiving average wage rates of £2 per week (although both were accommodated rent free). Contemporary reports make various estimates that are of little value as they fail to take into account work methodologies. Inglis, in 1834, believed that the wages of 'the boys and girls were from 2s.6d. to 7s. per week; the upgrown persons worked at task-work and might easily earn £1 per week'.[19] *The Waterford Chronicle* reported in 1839 that the wages averaged from 7s. to 35s. per week, with some obtaining 'even a higher sum than that'.[20] The Malcomsons themselves reported more accurate information. In an 1849 letter to factory inspector James Stewart the firm reported that the necessity of hiring an additional 135 workers would have added an extra £4,000 to the wage bill; suggesting an average wage of about 12s. per week.[21] The most reliable figure available is perhaps Joseph Malcomson's estimate of 1854 that the average price of labour for the firm was 'about 7s. a week.'[22]

The amount earned was in most of the factory departments determined by the operatives' own ability to perform the required tasks speedily and efficiently. Girls in the weaving shed were paid by piece rates, a system that worked to the benefit of the firm and

> the girl who keeps her loom clean and well oiled and in good order and who is watchful immediately to piece her thread if it breaks, will, at the end of the week, have more done than one who is less attentive.[23]

Robert Malcomson explained the background to the introduction of this method of payment. In Clonmel, they paid a weekly wage to each new worker but found that

> they did not give their attention to learn the trade. We then established the rule of allowing them to learn it at their own expense, and paid nothing, until they had earned it.[24]

William Malcomson explained his philosophy on this question to the members of the Portlaw Agricultural Society in October 1858, when he recommended the advantages of 'allowing the quantity of work to regulate the payment', to the farmers of the district. This system improved factory efficiency, worker performance and remuneration. If the Malcomsons as manufacturers had gone on the principle of payment by days worked,

> they would have had a factory double the size, and have double the number of hands to produce the quantity they were weekly turning out; but the workers would individually only receive half the wages they now earn.[25]

The firm had for

twenty-five years adopted the principle of endeavouring to make the labourer selfish, to make him feel that his own exertions, and his own remuneration went together.[26]

The standard of living enjoyed by the workers of the cotton town is more important than a consideration of the wages earned. Regularity of work and income per family was far higher than that achieved by workers in other disciplines or in surrounding regions. Family income in Portlaw was relatively high regardless of wages paid. The demand for labour in the factory ensured that wives, daughters and young persons would be in regular employment as well as the male head of households thus adding to the family income. The same earning opportunities did not present themselves in agriculture. In 1861, in county Waterford, a male farm labourer earned up to 2s. and a female 1s. daily but only during the harvest season. On all other occasions wealthy farmers hired day labourers at 10d. daily, without food. Women had no earnings by task except unloading colliers when their earnings averaged 2s.6d. weekly.[27]

Portlaw families also had the potential to add to their incomes by keeping lodgers in their houses. The census of 1841 recorded 193 male and 302 female visitors for the town.[28] This category of resident had increased to 342 male and 567 female by 1861.[29] The majority of these 'visitors' were people who had taken up residence in the town having obtained factory employment.

Employment trends at the Portlaw factory in the period 1835–74 can be examined using information contained in nine returns compiled at irregular intervals, by the factory inspectors. Although these returns are in some ways unsatisfactory they are the only official source of information on the employment history of the firm. Four major trends are identifiable for the period of study. First a period of continual growth between 1835[30]–56,[31] during which time the average annual rate of increase was c.4.0 per cent. Within this period the fastest rate of growth took place between 1835–8[32] when the number of operatives employed increased at an annual rate of 11.0 per cent.[33] This was followed by a 14 per cent decline in the number of employees from 1,648 to 1,412 between 1856[34] and 1862.[35] Thirdly there was an increase of similar proportions in the numbers employed between 1862 to 1867.[36] Finally the period between 1867 and 1870[37] saw an 11.3 per cent decline which had stabilised by 1874.[38] The company was involved in a major struggle to survive, ultimately to end in failure in 1876 as the firm became bankrupt.

The mechanisation of the process of transforming raw cotton into finished cloth had major implications for an industrial workforce. Firstly workers were employed to perform a variety of specific tasks; secondly most processes were reduced to routine machine minding and tending, the pace of which was largely determined by the speed and reliability of the technology. This task required operators to be alert and vigilant but demanded little in the way of skill and technique. Thirdly, it eliminated most heavy manual labour, enabling children and women to be employed to a degree that was un-paralleled in non-textile industries.[39] The result was, excluding 1838, a Portlaw labour force dominated by females and youths less than eighteen years of age.

The returns for 1836[40] and 1839[41] provide the most detailed information for the age and gender structure of the employees. Classifying the information into four categories namely males and females less than thirteen, thirteen to eighteen, eighteen to twenty-one and over twenty-one reveals the following pattern

Table 10 Age and sex structure, Portlaw cotton plant, 1835 and 1838

Year	per cent less than 13		per cent over 13 under 18		per cent over 18 under 21		per cent over 21	
	Male	*Female*	*Male*	*Female*	*Male*	*Female*	*Male*	*Female*
1835	4	3	18	25	6	14	9	22
1838	–	–	16	18	4	10	31	21

Source: R.I.F., 1836, p. 3; 1839, p. 335.

The 1835 workforce was a mainly young and female one, 64 per cent being female and 69 per cent aged less than 21. Three significant changes had taken place in the structure of the increased workforce by 1838. The percentage of operatives less than twenty-one years of age had decreased by 17 per cent to 52 per cent of the total. The number of adult male workers increased from sixty-three to 311 to form 31 per cent of the workforce and there was a slight overall majority of male workers.[42] Thirdly, children less than thirteen years of age were no longer employed having formed 7 per cent of the 1835 workforce.

The introduction of factory legislation and continued expansion at the Portlaw plant were significant influences on this changing pattern. Legislation requiring school attendance for factory children less than thirteen years of age was passed in August 1833.[43] From 1836 these children were required to attend school at least two hours per day and they were also restricted to working less than forty-eight hours in a single week and not more than nine hours any one day. This provision required factory owners to significantly increase the number of children employed to allow for the labour loss of the time spent at school, with the consequent inconvenience and increased administrative work for factory managers. The alternative was to employ older workers full time. This was the solution adopted by the Malcomson firm, and is confirmed by factory inspector James Stuart in his report for the half year ending 30 June 1839. According to Stuart Messrs. Malcomson were

> unwilling on their own account, and on account of the health of the
> children, to employ them until they had attained their thirteenth year,

the importunity of parents was such, that they were never able, until fortified by the provisions of the Act, to prevent the introduction of children into their factories.[44]

The 1830s were a period of great expansion in the firm (the second phase of the spinning section was completed by 1837).[45] and the associated construction work required the hiring of additional male labour. However the weaving extension was still in its construction stage by October 1839 where according to the *Waterford Chronicle* 'a large addition is making to the edifice'.[46] This necessitated the employment of a large number of skilled tradesmen and labourers and these were obviously included in the returns made to the factory inspectors.

After 1839 the factory exhibited a remarkable consistency in the overall gender balance of the workforce. The female employees in 1847,[47] 1850[48] and 1857[49] accounted for 57.97 per cent, 56.10 per cent and 55.95 per cent of the workforce respectively. The 1862 returns departed from this consistency with a 60.41 per cent female workforce.[50] The remaining three sets of returns of 1867,[51] 1871[52] and 1875[53] restored the pattern of consistency although with a lesser proportion of female workers – 52.42 per cent, 53.77 per cent and 52.61 per cent respectively (Table 11).

The labour force was restructured in the 1860s. In 1862 young males and females per had replaced 10 per cent of the adult male work force, a decrease of 220 numerically. This structural change was related to development work taking place in the Portlaw village. This was a time of major building developments in the town as illustrated in the second chapter. This work was in full progress in 1862.[54] It is most likely that members of the adult male factory workforce were redirected to this construction work. The bulk of the work was completed in the early 1860s and in the 1867[55] and 1871[56] returns the balance was restored, with *c.*33 per cent of the workforce made up of males aged eighteen or greater, with the percentage of females reduced to *c.*50 per cent and the adolescent males (13–18 years) to *c.*9 per cent.

There was a radical shift in policy in relation to the employment of children (under thirteen) after 1862. These were the 'half timers,' and this category ranged in importance from 7 to 10 per cent in the years 1867–74. Factory legislation required these children to attend school for a certain number of hours each day and they were required to present a certificate at the beginning of each working week confirming their school attendance. This was a period of economic difficulty for the firm and the probability is that children were re-employed at this time as a cost cutting measure. Wage rates may also have been reduced for adult operatives so that parental pressure resulting from a drop in overall income may have necessitated children returning to mill employment.

Table 11 Age structure of operatives, Portlaw cotton factory, 1835–74 (%)

	1835	1838	1847	1850	1856	1862	1867	1870	1874
Children under-13	7.22						7.62	7.96	9.74
Males 13–18	17.72	16.12	13.08	12.26	12.07	17.85	9.39	8.37	13.25
Females 13+	60.35	48.97	57.97	56.10	55.95	60.41	50.09	50.31	47.94
Males 18+	14.71	34.91	28.95	31.64	31.98	21.74	32.9	33.36	29.07

Source: R.I.F., 1836, p. .3; 1839, p. 335; 1847, p. 8; 1850, p. 10; 1857 p. 16. 1862, p.19; 1867–8; p. 23; 1871, p.71; 1875, p.7.

A number of significant differences emerge between the structure of the Portaw workforce and the national one. Nationally females formed a higher proportion of the workforce than they did at Portlaw. Secondly, the numbers of adult males (over 18) employed nationally averaged 18 per cent while the corresponding Portlaw figure was 29 per cent.

Outside of Portlaw the cotton industry was based in the large urban centres of Belfast and Dublin where competition for labour was intense. Male labour would not have been as easily or as cheaply sourced and would have been far more costly than female labour. The Portlaw industry developed on an abandoned milling site in an area with no tradition of textile industry. There was little competition for labour, costs were therefore far lower and so the necessity for cheap female labour was not a priority. The integrated nature of the Portlaw plant together with the ancillary workshops and foundry increased the requirement for adult male labour and would have reduced the proportion of females in the workforce. A third difference was the absence of children from the national workforce after 1838 whereas they formed an average of 8 per cent of the workforce at Portlaw in the period 1865–74. Some reasons have been already suggested for this difference.

Little evidence is available concerning the early marketing strategy of the factory. According to Marmion writing in 1858 the trade 'commenced by supplying a few shops in Waterford and Clonmel'.[57] Robert Malcomson explained the relationship between the hand weaving factory in Clonmel and the early Portlaw spinning mill. The handloom factory in Clonmel remained in operation to consume part of the extra yarn produced at Portlaw.[58] Surviving business accounts give some insight into the marketing strategy of

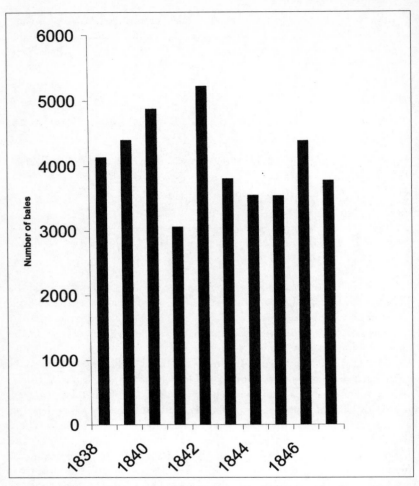

15. Bales of cotton imported via Waterford port by Malcomson brothers, 1838-47.
Source: Waterford Newsletter, 1838–47.

the factory in the early 1830s. At this stage the firm had not yet developed a major export market. Calico was sold mainly to Irish firms with less frequent consignments going to Britain. This is confirmed by Lewis who reported that the 'cottons are bleached on the premises, and are sold chiefly in the home markets, though large quantities are sometimes sent to America'.[59] The trade figures reported thrice weekly in the *Waterford Newsletter* are the only detailed source of information on the trading pattern of the firm from 1838–47. The newspaper records the amount of cotton imported in bales (Figure 15) with calico exports recorded in bales and boxes (Figure 16). These figures indicate the increased importance of the export market especially after 1843.

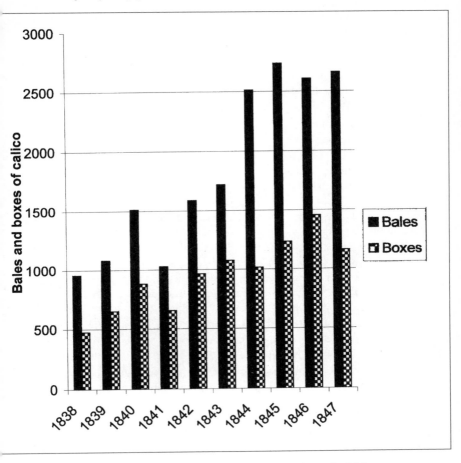

16. Bales and boxes of cotton exported from Waterford port by Malcomson Brothers 1838–47. *Source: Waterford Newsletter*, 1838–47.

The dependence on the home market had changed by the end of the 1830s and this expertise in identifying and cultivating foreign markets was crucial to the success of the Malcomson cotton enterprise. J.F. Maguire, visited Portlaw, organising material for the national industrial exhibition of 1852 and found the proprietors disinterested in taking part, such was their dependence on foreign markets. According to Maguire 'hundreds of immense bails were forwarded weekly to all parts of the civilised and uncivilised world'. Cotton manufactured in Portlaw was marketed in the 'eastern archipelago, in

Hindostan and China, in Mexico, the West Indies, Brazil' and on 'the west coast from Cape Horn to Oregon'. Maguire reported that 42,000 pounds of cotton were weekly manufactured into calico, producing a weekly average of 120,000 yards.[60] The reported weekly consumption of cotton was more than the total national import of cotton in 1800 and the company investment in Portlaw claimed to be £100,000 in 1847, was roughly one-third of the total fixed capital of the entire Irish cotton industry in 1800.[61]

Cotton was imported and exported to and from the port of Waterford by scheduled steamers via Liverpool from where it was exported to the various world markets in which the firm traded. The normal carrier company was the Waterford Commercial and Steamship Navigation company. Not surprisingly the long commercial arm of the Malcomson family stretched deep into this company, which was incorporated on 13 July 1835, with a share capital of £97,000 made up of 970 ordinary shares. 247 of these shares were purchased by members of the Malcomson family[62] and as the century progressed additional shares were purchased.[63] The family also serviced the river Plate trade from Liverpool. The *Cordova, Parana, Paraguay, Uruguay, La Plata* and *Una* were advertised as being dispatched monthly to the river Plate, journeying directly from Liverpool to Montevideo and Buenos Aires.[64] Not only were the Malcomson ship-owners but many of the ships had been built at their own shipbuilding yard in Waterford.[65] This connection with commercial steamship companies reduced the cost of exporting cotton goods from Portlaw and eliminated many problems arising from the geographic location of the plant.

The American civil war presented serious problems for the British cotton industry. The Malcomson firm in Portlaw made significant adjustments to its work practices to cope with the difficulties created by the general shortage of raw cotton supplies. Remarkably employment numbers increased by 15 per cent from 1,412[66] to 1,620[67] between 1862 and 1867. Apart from attempting to beat the blockade imposed by Union forces, the firm imported linen yarns and wool to maintain production levels and while a contemporary newspaper reported that the concerns were not at full work, 'they have managed to keep the hands very fairly employed'.[68] William Malcomson claimed 'that five hundred hands were in their establishment in the flax manufacture alone' in September 1864.[69] A newspaper report of 1865 is more detailed on the factory adjustments to deal with changing circumstances. Linen weaving was introduced requiring machinery alteration. Yarn was purchased from Messrs. Russell of Limerick and in Belfast. The adjustments were so successful that the factory could bring over a number of starving operatives from Lancashire.[70] William Malcomson, referred to these developments when addressing the members of the Iverk Agricultural Society in October 1865. 'Necessity had driven his firm to provide the best machinery,' and his firm had never destroyed so much machinery during the twenty-five years of his intimate connection with it, in the same period of time as within that last three or four years. The firm found that the machinery it employed was not able to manufacture at profit and consequently it displaced it and introduced new machinery in its stead, which with inferior material, produced a larger amount of results.[71]

It is clear that the firm's specialisation in cotton manufacturing was ended by the early 1860s. This was reflected in the variety of cloth that the firm exhibited at the Dublin exhibition of 1864. Specimens of 'indigo ticken cotton, blue Denim's platilla, slate Denims platilla, grey and white shirting, cotton mixed poplin, linen and all possible makes of linen and calico', were displayed.[72] The extent of the change is also reflected in the 1871 census which has detailed information on the structure of the Portlaw workforce.[73] 170 male weavers were categorised, seventy-five classified as weavers of mixed fabrics[74] and 201 of the 427 female weavers worked with mixed fabrics.[75]

The *Waterford Newsletter* trade statistics are also available from 1869 to the collapse of the firm in 1876 (Figures 17 and 18). The information is not as easily interpreted as the information from the 1840s for a number of reasons. During this period imports were serving linen factories in Carrick-on-Suir and Clonmel as well as the Portlaw factory.

Apart from raw cotton, bales of tow, yarn, flax, hemp and jute were imported in varying quantities without specifying their ultimate destination. Exports were measured in bales and boxes without identifying the material involved. The figures are however useful in illustrating a number of points of importance in relation to the firm's final years. The difference in the quantities of cotton imported in the 1840s and 1870s was insignificant. The large volumes of tow imported suggest a change of emphasis on the part of the firm moving from producing calico cloth in great quantities to lower value produce. Tow is the waste produced following the completion of the carding process in the preparation of flax prior to spinning. It was used to spin coarser yarns and for weaving heavier fabrics such as sacking and also twisted and used for ropes manufacturing.[76] Hemp and jute were also imported and used for producing similar products. Low value rope, twine, sacking and roofing felt featured in the lists of exports from Malcomson Brothers in the 1870s.[77] The export figures quantify the decline in the export trade after 1872 and its sharp fall in 1876.

Space constraints permit only the briefest examination of the final collapse of the Malcomson business empire. Malcomson Brothers, by the very nature of the cotton industry and their diverse range of business interests, were participants in the global economy and from the late 1830s depended on the export market for their success. The 1870s were a time of economic depression worldwide impacting particularly on the core Malcomson business. The slump

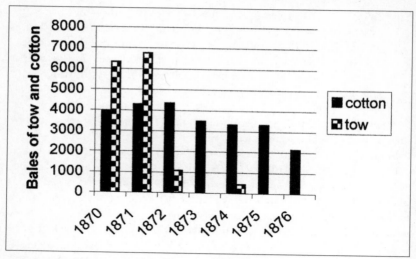

17. Bales of cotton and tow imported via Waterford port by Malcomson brothers, 1870–76. Source: *Waterford Newsletter*, 1870–76.

in international trade had obvious repercussions on shipping and in 1876 their London steamship enterprises had accumulated losses of £67,757.[78] Linen manufacturing, a branch of the textile industry in which the Malcomsons made considerable investments in the 1860s, suffered a serious slump in the 1870s. World cotton prices also began a period of decline in 1873 that lasted for the rest of the century. This originated in a relative decline in demand worldwide combined with an over expansion of supply.[79] The Malcomson cotton business, having survived the cotton famine and the problems caused by the American Civil War, was unable to withstand this crisis and an 'experiment' of fifty years finally ended in the court of bankruptcy. Liabilities amounted to £551,894 with combined assets of £202,094, in the statement of affairs of Malcomsom Brothers presented to the creditors in June 1876.[80]

The performance of the Portlaw cotton industry with its 1860s adjustments defied the national trend. Nationally the industry was unimportant following its era of success between the 1780s and 1820s. The Portlaw industry, by contrast, enjoyed continual success during the period of study, with employment never falling below 1,000 after 1838. The labour force was dominated by females and young adults with the industry sustained by concentrating on foreign markets. The final years of the business seem to have been a struggle for survival, a struggle that finally ended in June 1876. Portlaw deprived of its sustaining life force went into immediate decline.

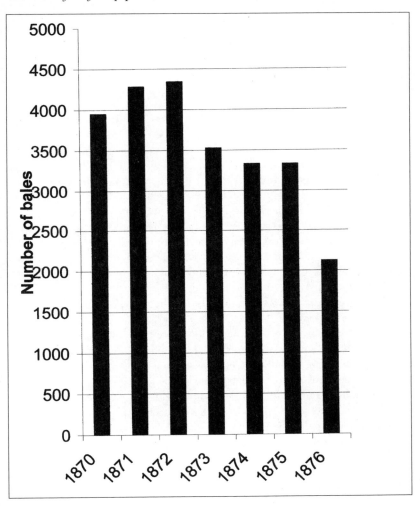

18. Bales of merchandise exported from Waterford port by Malcomson brothers, 1870–75. Source: *Waterford Newsletter,* 1870–75.

Conclusion

The most obvious conclusion to be drawn from this study is that from 1826 until the early 1860s the cotton industry survived and flourished in Portlaw and continued as a mixed textile business until 1876. The performance of the Portlaw cotton industry defied the national trend. Nationally the industry was in continuous decline, a process that was reversed by the occasional short lived venture, such as the weaving industry that flourished briefly at Drogheda in the 1860s. The Portlaw industry, by contrast, enjoyed continual success during the period of study, with employment never falling below 1,000 after 1838, until bankruptcy in 1876. Problems caused by raw cotton shortages, due to the American Civil War, were overcome in the 1860s by the introduction of linen spinning and weaving to the plant so that from the early 1860s mixed fabrics were produced as well as cotton goods. The scale of this change was such that 46 per cent of the weavers employed in 1871 worked on mixed fabrics.[1]

The cotton industry was of minor importance nationally during the period under review. The industry had enjoyed its greatest period of strength between the 1780s and the 1820s but with a few exceptions failed to expand in the later decades. The number of working factories declined from twenty-eight in 1835, to eight in 1874, with numbers employed falling from 4,622 in 1838 to 3,075 in 1874. Excluding Portlaw, cotton manufacturing employed only 1,600 nationally in 1874. The weakness of the Irish cotton industry resulted from the slow introduction of powerlooms and the consequent exclusion of Irish cotton goods from the export market. Hand woven Irish cotton goods could not compete with mechanically woven, better quality, cheaper mass produced goods.[2] The opposite situation prevailed in Portlaw. The rapid introduction of powerlooms predated similar developments in Britain and a sophisticated and geographically diverse foreign market had been developed by the late 1830s. These developments helped to sustain the industry in Portlaw for exactly half of the nineteenth century.

The wonder is not that the Portlaw industry virtually collapsed in 1876 but that it vigorously survived to that date. The concentration on foreign markets allied to the fully integrated and self-sufficient nature of the plant were important. The fact that the plant was part of a much larger multi-faceted commercial conglomerate was also important and profits from other elements of the business may have been used to cross-finance the Portlaw plant and tide it over times of recession. The Malcomson business empire included a large mercantile marine element with Malcomson ships used to ferry the cotton to many of its worldwide destinations. This helped to offset the impact of additional transport costs incurred due to the geographic isolation of Portlaw. Not only were Malcomson ships used to transport the cotton goods and several of these ships were built in the family's Neptune shipbuilding yard at Waterford.

The Portlaw cotton industry was labour intensive and vertically integrated involving spinning, weaving, a variety of finishing processes and several ancillary activities designed to support the primary business. Over the period of study the proportion of females employed was in a slight majority (56 per cent), whereas nationally the proportion of female employment over the same period was 72 per cent. This was influenced by the variety of trades practiced at Portlaw, the all embracing nature of the plant where finishing, loading and unloading required male labour and the rural location of the plant where the reduced competition for labour helped to keep wage rates low.

The developments at Portlaw were the responsibility of three different members of the Malcomson family, each making significant contributions to the overall development. The economic vision, entrepreneurial vigor and acumen of David Malcomson was responsible for establishing the industry and associated town. Living in Clonmel at a defining moment in the history of the milling industry and benefiting from the town's well-established Quaker business network, he earned a considerable fortune as a miller and flour exporter. Sensitive to the changed political circumstances of the 1820s and their damaging impact on grain prices and apprehension about the perceived repeal of the corn laws encouraged him to seek an alternative business opportunity. Portlaw, because of its waterpower potential, was chosen as the location for what became the success story of the Irish cotton industry. David Malcomson retired from the business in 1838 and was replaced by his son Joseph as the managing partner. Joseph was responsible for the rapid expansion of the powerloom weaving section of the business and for the identification and development of reliable foreign markets. Following his sudden death in 1858 Joseph Malcomson was succeeded by his brother William as managing partner. William supervised the radical redevelopment of the town of Portlaw. His decision to introduce linen spinning and weaving and the manufacture of mixed fabrics was instrumental in guiding the plant through the difficult era of the American Civil War and the consequent cotton famine. Unfortunately, he was also the chief partner when economic circumstances conspired to cause the collapse of what was then a major multi-faceted, multi-national business empire.

Industrial villages as explained previously developed in two phases. The earliest villages were purpose built to attract workers to rural areas with water power potential. Later nineteenth-century developments were designed by wealthy, socially conscious capitalists who decided to move from squalid urban environs and re-locate on green-field sites and provide workers with a more congenial physical and social environment.

Developments at Portlaw embraced both these phases. The original development by David Malcomson was necessary to provide the infrastructure for the factory operatives. Workers were attracted to Portlaw by the construction of decent quality houses and gradually over time a social infrastructure evolved, which encouraged some to describe the town as a model village. This suggests an overall plan or ideology on the part of the founder, similar in nature to that of James Richardson, who shaped Bessbrook to meet the requirements of his social and economic vision or that of W. H. Lever's model industrial village of Port Sunlight founded in 1888. The reality, in Portlaw, was somewhat different, as the original development was more piecemeal in nature until the town was radically redesigned in the late 1850s and early 1860s. Most of this work was carried out when William Malcomson was the managing partner. Unlike, later developments by Titus Salt, W.H. Lever or the Cadburys he avoided moving to a green-field site by demolishing Mulgrave and Shamrock Streets and used the open space created to totally rebuild the core area of the town. This radical intervention was followed by a single sustained building programme based on a unitary design plan. The triangular form of the street morphology, the regular plot patterns, the long straight wide streets and the similarity of house design generated in Portlaw a sense of uniformity, spaciousness and order that is rare in Irish small towns.

This study has made a significant contribution to our understanding of the history of the development of the small town in Ireland and in particular to our knowledge of the working of the rarely studied phenomenon of the Irish industrial village. Graham and Proudfoot argued that the 'the era of urban improvement was more or less complete by 1840, its last anachronistic impulse occurring on the Trinity College estate in Kerry where Caherciveen was largely a product of the 1860s'.[3] Portlaw can now be included in the list of towns benefiting from late nineteenth-century redevelopment.

The provision of welfare and social institutions were an essential element of the Portlaw infrastructure. These were best developed during William Malcomson's tenure. We have some knowledge of his social philosophies. He was a firm believer in the value of education and an advocate of providing workers with quality housing but these views were as rooted in utilitarianism as they were in mid-Victorian paternalism or Quaker inspired benevolence. The primary motive of the Malcomson Portlaw development was profit accumulation. The elaborate social structure constructed by the family was not only desirable in itself but was also good for business. The provision of decent housing originally, and superior housing in the second phase of the town's development, was a powerful device for recruiting, stabilising and controlling a workforce. Education provision was not designed to lead to upward mobility or future prosperity but to produce a more efficient operative. William Malcomson, was in no doubt about this. In 1871 he explained that

> the man who can both work and think was able to produce more in any employment than the uneducated worker. If they had not an educated class of labourers they could not get a fair day's work from the machinery.[4]

A congenial working environment, a strong emphasis on temperance and provision for health care and a general sense of purpose and community fostered by regular company outings led to efficient profitable production.

However this is only part of the story. The Portlaw development bore the indelible stamp of a nineteenth-century Quaker enterprise and the range of social provision available was a distinguishing feature of many contemporary British Quaker enterprises. The Quakers were, during the eighteenth and nineteenth centuries a society of plain-dealing people noted for their honesty. Their strong sense of individualism led to a respect for the essential rights and dignity of others that was expressed by the adoption of various worthy causes and to Quaker business enterprises being underpinned by a strong moral code. The term 'enlightened self-interest' perhaps best describes the link between Quaker ethics and business interests.[5] In Portlaw, the Quaker influence was enriched considerably by the zeal of the factory doctor James Martin who was a tireless champion of the virtue of self-improvement.

Portlaw, whose economic and social well being depended on the viability of the industry, suffered serious difficulties following the industry's collapse. The most obvious manifestation of the problems was a sharp decline in population (Table 14).

Table 14. Population change in Portlaw 1841–1901

Population: Portlaw 1841–1901						
1841	*1851*	*1861*	*1871*	*1881*	*1891*	*1901*
3,647	4,351	3,852	3,774	1,891	1,394	1,101

Economic decline and stagnation found vivid representation in the decayed physical fabric of the town so evocatively portrayed by David Wark, a Presbyterian minister from Waterford city who visited the town in 1900:

> An indescribably dreary effect is produced by these long rows of houses, with windows boarded up, and stuck over with a patchwork of

advertisements in various stages of decay, or with gaping holes where
the glass has broken away, while off the outsides the plaster has fallen
in great patches, giving the walls the appearance of having been attacked
by some devastating skin disease.[6]

Deprived of the *raison d'être* for its existence, the mills, Portlaw was now a
pitiful shadow of the town that had so impressed a range of visitors such as
Binns, the Halls and Inglis in the 1830s. The essence of the decay was perfectly
captured by Wark:

> One wants to get away as speedily as possible from such depressing
> surroundings.[7]

Notes

ABBREVIATIONS

B.I.G.S.	*Bulletin of the Irish Georgian Society*
E.H.R.	*Economic History Review*
F.I.R.	*Reports of inspectors of factories*
I.H.S.	*Irish Historical Studies*
I.E.S.H.	*Irish Economic and Social History*
J.R.S.A.I.	*Journal of the Royal Society of Antiquaries of Ireland*
L.E.C.	Landed estates commission, National Archives
N.A.	National Archives
N.L.I.	National Library of Ireland
O.P.W.	Offices of Public Works
O.S.	Ordnance Survey
P.H.S.	Presbyterian Historical Society
R. D.	Registry of Deeds
R.I.F.	*Returns of inspectors of factories*
S.F.I.L.	Society of Friends in Ireland Library, Dublin
V.O.	Valuation Office
W.M.	*Waterford Mail*
W.L.	William Lawrence
W.M.L.	Waterford Municipal Library

INTRODUCTION

1 Cormac Ó Gráda, *Ireland, a new economic history 1780–1939* (Oxford, 1994), pp 278–82.

2 Margaret T. Fogarty, 'The Malcomsons and the economic development of the lower Suir valley, 1782–1877,' (Unpublished M.Sc. thesis U.C.C., 1968).

3 Majella Walshe, 'Portlaw: a model industrial village,' (Unpublished Masters thesis in urban and building conservation, U.C.D., 1995).

4 A. P. Williamson, 'Enterprise, industrial development, and social planning: Quakers and the emergence of the textile industry in Ireland' in *Planning Perspectives*, vii, (1992), pp 303–328.

5 Desmond G. Neill, *Portlaw, a nineteenth century Quaker enterprise based on a model village* (Dublin, 1992).

6 P. Power, 'The Portlaw cotton factory' in *Waterford and South East Ireland Archaeology Society Journal*, xii, (1910), pp 58–65.

7 Power, 'The Portlaw cotton factory,' p. 59.

8 Denis Stewart Macneice, 'Factory workers' housing in counties Down and Armagh,' (unpublished Ph. D thesis, Queen's University Belfast), 1981, (hereafter 'Workers' housing').

9 Denis Macneice, 'Industrial villages of Ulster, 1800–1900', in P. Roebuck, (ed.), *Plantation to Partition* (Belfast, 1981) pp 172–190.

10 N.A., Copy ledger of Malcomson's mill, Portlaw county Waterford,

1795–98 and 1830–35, Business records, Waterford 8, (hereafter Business records).

11 N.A., Document relating to the property and interests of the Malcomson family, 975/14/1–10.

12 O.S., _County Waterford, sheet 8, 1:10,560_, surveyed in 1841, engraved in 1842.

13 O.S., _County Waterford, sheet 8, 1:10,560_, surveyed in 1905, published in 1907.

14 V.O., Valuation lists, number 8, county of Waterford, county health district of Waterford, electoral division of Portlaw, Carrick-on-Suir, number 2, 1855–68 (hereafter Valuation lists).

15 V.O., Field survey book, county of Waterford, barony of Upperthird, parish of Clonegam, (hereafter Field survey book).

16 N.A., Perambulation book of the parish of Clonegam, including the town of Portlaw, in the barony of Upperthird, county Waterford. OL 4.3479 (hereafter Perambulation book).

17 N.A., Valuation office, house books, Portlaw, County Waterford, OL 5.3390–3 (hereafter House books).

18 N.L.I., _Malcomson family memoir_, Microfilm p. 6935.

19 Peter Solar, 'The agricultural trade of the port of Waterford 1809–1909', in William Nolan, Thomas P. Power (eds.), _Waterford history & society: interdisciplinary essays on the history of an Irish county_ (Dublin, 1992) p. 496.

RURAL CLUSTER TO PLANNED INDUSTRIAL VILLAGE

1 W Ashworth, 'British industrial villages in the nineteenth century,' in _E.H.R._, iii, (1951), pp 378–387.

2 C. Fell Smith, _James N. Richardson of Bessbrook_, (London, 1925), p. 49.

3 Macneice, 'Workers' housing', p. 61.

4 Macneice, 'Workers' housing', pp 1–3.

5 N.A., Business records, Waterford 8.

6 R.D., 497/97/317966.

7 R.D., 1822/777/249/526384.

8 T. Hunt, 'The origin and development of the Portlaw cotton industry,' in _Decies_, no. 53, (1997), p. 19.

9 Kenneth Charlton, 'The state of Ireland in the 1820s, James Cropper's plan,' in _I.H.S._ iv, (1971) pp 320–39.

10 S.F.I.L., Copy of letter from David Malcomson to Richard Ussher, 18 April 1825, Port.76.

11 R.D., 802/6/541141.

12 R.D., 802/5/541140.

13 R.D., 654/622/452349.

14 R.D., 654/623/452350

15 _W.M._, 12 January 1825.

16 De LaTocnaye, _A Frenchman's walk through Ireland 1796–7_, translated from the French of De LaTocnaye by John Stevenson, 1917, with an introduction by John A. Gamble, (Belfast, 1984), p. 68.

17 _Malcomson Memoir_.

18 N.A. Perambulation book, OL4.3479, p. 107.

19 _The Preston Temperance Advocate_, July 1837, p.52.

20 N.A., V.O., No. 2 house book, OL5.3391, pp 31–44.

21 Ibid., pp 31–44.

22 _Primary valuation of tenements, county of Waterford, barony of Upperthird, parish of Clonagam_, (Dublin, 1850), p. 10 (hereafter _Primary valuation of tenements_).

23 N.A. _V.O._, No. 2 house book, OL5.3391, pp 28–30.

24 R.D., 1834/20/27.

25 N.A.VO., No. 2 house book, OL5.3393, pp 45–58.

26 N.A., V.O., No. 1 house book, OL5.3390, pp 4–11.

27 N.A.,V.O., No.1 house book, OL5.3390, pp 34–54.

28 V.O. Field survey book, pp 59–65.

29 N.A., No. 1 house book, OL5.3390, pp 62–69.

30 R.D., 649/498/452351; 654/622/452349; 654/623/452350; 722/307/493442.

31 N.A.,V. O., No. 2 house book, OL5.3393, pp 20–32.

32 L.E.C.,Abstract of title of John Thomas Medlycott Esq. to lands of Mayfield and others in barony of Upperthird, county Waterford, box 301, EC 2180.

33 *Primary valuation of tenements*, pp 2–3; 13–14.

34 *Waterford Chronicle,* 8 October 1839.

35 N.A.,V.O., No. 2, house book, OL5.3391, p. 20.

36 *Primary valuation of the several tenements*, pp 2–11.

37 *Census of Ireland*, p. 368, H.C., 1852–3, xci.499.

38 *Appendix to the report of the select committee on the county cess (Ireland) with the minutes of evidence, appendix and index*, appendix no.3, p. 21, H.C. 1836 (527), xii. The quality index used by Richard Griffith is explained in his evidence to the committee.

39 Mr & Mrs S. C. Hall, *Ireland: its scenery, character, &c*, (London, 1842), p. 310 .

40 H. Inglis, *Ireland in 1834, a journey through Ireland during the spring, summer and autumn of 1834,* (2 vols, London, 1834), i, pp 72–4.

41 *F.I.R.*, July-December 1842, p. 18, H.C. 1843 [429], xxvii, 289.

42 B.J.Graham and L.J. Proudfoot, *Urban improvement in provincial Ireland, 1700–1840*, (Athlone,1994), pp 3–12 (hereafter *Urban improvement*).

43 *Urban improvement*, p. 23.

44 *Census of Ireland, 1851*, p. 356.

45 R.D., 1852/21/14; 1852/21/15.

46 *W. M.*, 27 October 1862.

47 *W.M.*, 27 October 1862.

48 R.D., 1870/22/180.

49 F. O'Dwyer, 'John Skipton Mulvaney, Architect, 1813–70', in *B.I.G.S.* 1988, p. 40–1.

50 V.O.,Valuation lists, number 8, 1855–68.

51 Valuation lists, number 8, 1855–68.

52 Valuation lists, number 8, 1855–68.

53 Valuation lists, number 8, 1855–68.

54 Valuation lists, number 8, 1855–68.

55 *W.M.*, 31 October 1862.

56 *W.M.*, 31 October 1862.

57 *W.M.*, 5 December 1862.

58 *W.M.*, 5 October 1871.

59 *W.M.*, 31 October 1862.

60 E.D. Mapother, 'The unhealthiness of Irish towns and the want of sanitary legislation,' in *Journal of the statistical and social inquiry society of Ireland*, part xxxi, (January 1866), p. 161.

THE SOCIAL WORLD OF THE VILLAGE

1 Arthur E. J.Went, 'The cardboard tokens of Malcomson Brothers of Portlaw county Waterford', in *J.R.S.A.I.*, xcviii, (1968), pp 75–78.

2 *Malcomson Memoir*.

3 *Slater's national commercial directory of Ireland*, (Manchester and Dublin, 1846), p. 303.

4 *Slater's royal national commercial directory of Ireland*, (Manchester and London, 1870), p. 198.

5 Information obtained from an analysis of the Valuation Office house books.

6 *W.M.*, 21 August 1871.

7 *Malcomson Memoir*.

8 F.I.R., *31 October 1842*, p. 14, 1843, [429] xxvii, 289.

9 J.F.Maguire, *The industrial movement in Ireland as illustrated by the national*

exhibition of 1852, (London,1853),
pp 166–7.

10   Maguire, *Industrial movement*,
     pp 166–7.

11   Maguire, *Industrial movement*,
     pp 166–7.

12   Elizabeth Malcolm, '*Ireland sober,
     Ireland free'; drink and temperance in
     nineteenth-century Ireland*, (Syracuse,
     1986), pp 56–66.

13   Henry Corby, *Irish medical directory*,
     (Dublin, 1846).

14   Malcolm, *Ireland sober*, p. 88.

15   *The Preston Temperance Advocate*, July
     1837, p. 52.

16   *Malcomson Memoir.*

17   *Malcomson Memoir.*

18   W. C., 8 October 1839.

19   W.C., 8 October 1839.

20   F.I.R.., *July-December 1841*, p. 23,
     H.C. 1842 [31], xxii, 337.

21   F.I.R., *July-December 1842*, p. 14,
     H.C. 1843 [503], xxvii, 289.

22   *Malcomson Memoir.*

23   N.A., Copy will and probate David
     Malcomson, 2 February 1842,
     975/14/1.

24   42 Geo., III, cap.73. *Act for the
     preservation of the health and morals of
     apprentices and others employed in
     cotton and other mills and cotton and
     other factories*, 1802.

25   Michael Sanderson, 'Education and
     the factory in industrial Lancashire,
     1780–1840', in *E.H.R.*, xx (1967),
     p. 267.

26   *W.M.*, 5 October 1871.

27   Richard Lalor Sheil, *Sketches legal
     and political by the late right
     honourable Richard Lalor Sheil*,
     edited with notes by M.W. Savage
     esq., (London, 1855), p. 358.

28   *Second report of the commissioners of
     public instruction, Ireland*, (47) H.C.,
     1835, xxiv, p.13c.

29   Jonathan Binns, *The miseries and
     beauties of Ireland*, (2 vols, London,
     1837), ii, p. 427.

30   Maguire, *Industrial movement*, p. 166.

31   Slater L, *National commercial directory
     of Ireland*, (Manchester and
     Dublin,1846), p.303.

32   N.A., Ed.,1/87/ 22.

33   N.A., Ed.,1/87/54.

34   *F.I.R., 31 October 1868*, H.C., insert
     facing page 232,1868–69 [4093–1],
     xiv.123.

35   N.A., Ed.,1/87/22.

36   N.A., Ed.,2/183/91.

37   N.A., Ed.,1/87/59.

38   N.A., Ed., 2/183/91.

39   *W.M.*, 24 November 1865.

40   N.A. Ed., 9/2601.

41   N.A., Ed., 2/183/89.

42   N.A., Ed., 2/183/107.

43   N.A., Ed., 1/87/113.

44   Cohen Marilyn, *Linen, family, and
     community in Tullylish, county Down*,
     1690–1914, (Dublin, 1997), p. 168.

45   Marilyn Cohen, 'Paternalism and
     poverty: contradictions in the
     schooling of working-class children
     in Tullylish, county Down,
     1852–1914', in *History of Education*,
     xxi (1992), p. 299.

46   N.A., Ed., 1/87/27.

47   N.A., Ed., 1/87/27.

48   *Report of the assistant commissioners
     appointed to inquire into the nature and
     extent of the instruction afforded by the
     several institutions in Ireland for the pur-
     pose of elementary or primary education*,
     vol.II, p. 310, 1870 [C.6–1], xxviii,
     part ii, 381. (Hereafter *Powis report*).

49   *Ibid.*, p. 311.

50   Cohen, *Tullylish*, p. 169.

51   Cohen, 'Paternalism', p. 297.

52   *F.I.R., 31 October 1868*, insert facing
     page 232, H.C. 1868–69 [4093–1], xiv.

53   Cohen, *Tullylish*, p. 169.

54   *Census of Ireland for the year 1841*,
     p. xxxii, H.C. 1843, xxiv, 1.

55   *Census 1841*, p. xxxii.

56   W.Vaughan and J. Fitzpatrick (eds),
     *Irish historical statistics: population,
     1821–1971*, (Dublin, 1978), p. 34.

57 *Waterford Mirror*, 9 April 1830.

58 *W.M.*, 22 April 1863.

59 *W.M.*, 24 April 1864.

60 *W.M.*, 11 May 1866.

61 *W.M.*, 7 January 1876, 3 March 1876.

62 *W.M.*, 25 August 1871.

63 *W.M.*, 22 April 1863.

64 *W.M.*, 27 April 1864.

65 David Hempton and Myrtle Hill, 'Godliness and good citizenship': Evangelical protestantism and social control in Ulster, 1790–1850, in *Saothar*, xiii, (1988), pp 68–79.

66 *W.M.*, 27 April 1864.

67 *W.M.*, 27 April 1864.

68 *W.M.*, 26 February 1869.

69 *W.M.*, 22 April 1863.

70 *W.M.*, 17, 22, February 1865.

71 *W.M.*, 27 April 1864.

72 David Burns Windsor, *The Quaker Enterprise*, (London, 1980), p.111.

73 *W.M.*, 30 December 1864.

74 *W.M.*, 18 May 1863.

75 *W.M.*, 6 July 1865.

76 *WM.*, 6 July 1865.

77 *Waterford Chronicle*, 27 August 1869.

78 *W.M.*, 22 November 1867.

79 *W.M.*, 22 November 1867.

80 *W.M.*, 22 November 1867.

81 *W.M.*, 22 November 1867.

82 *W.M.*, 22 November 1867.

83 *W.M.*, 14 November 1856.

84 *W.M.*, 18 August 1869.

85 *W.M.*, 22 November 1867.

86 James Walvin, *The Quakers – money and morals*, (London, 1997), p. 57.

87 Walvin, *The Quakers, money and morals*, p.187.

88 Hempton and Hill, 'Godliness', p. 71.

89 *Waterford Chronicle*, 5 October 1839.

THE WORLD OF THE FACTORY: PHYSICAL STRUCTURE, POWER, PLANT AND EQUIPMENT

1 *W.M.*, 20 July 1825.

2 Lalor Sheil, *Sketches legal and political,* i, p. 360.

3 *Malcomson Memoir.*

4 Samuel Lewis, *A topographical dictionary of Ireland* (2 vols, London, 1836), ii, p. 466.

5 Mike Williams with D.A.Fairnie, *Cotton mills in greater Manchester,* (Preston, 1992), p. 54.

6 R.E. Jacob, *Quakers in industry and engineering in Ireland in the nineteenth century,* (unpublished, 1988), typescript in S.F.I.L. Details of measurement used in this chapter are those included in Jacob's typescript in the chapter entitled, 'notes on the construction of old cotton factory at Portlaw', by T. G. Kiely, p.20. Kiely was an architecht in the Portlaw tannery, which occupied part of the cotton factory from the 1930s–1980s where he carried out a detailed examination and measurement of the building.

7 Williams and Fairnie, *Cotton mills,* p. 80.

8 Geoffrey Timmins, *Four centuries of Lancashire cotton,* (Preston, 1996), p. 54.

9 Jacob, *Quakers in industry,* p. 23.

10 *Second report of evidence from the select committee on the state of the poor in Ireland, minutes of evidence,* pp 73–4, H.C. 1830 (654),vii.

11 *R.I.F.,* p. 19, H.C., 1862 (23) lv, 629.

12 *R.I.F.,* p. 23, H.C., 1867–8 (453) lxiv, 811, (data collected in 1867).

13 W.A.McCutcheon, 'The use of documentary source material in the Northern Ireland survey of industrial archaeology', in *E.H.R.,* xix (1966), p. 406.

14 Williams and Farnie, *Cotton mills,* pp 66, 83, 129.

15 *W.M.*, 14, 21 June, 5 July 1856.

16 *W.M.*, 14, 22 January 1876.

17 *W.M.*, 22 January 1876.

18 *W.M.*, 14 January 1876.

19 *W.M.*, 14 January 1876.

20 *W.M.*, 22 January 1876.

21 *W.M.*, 14 January 1876.

22   *W.M.*, 14 January 1876.

23   *W.M.*, 14 January 1876

24   Sidney Pollard, 'The factory village in the industrial revolution', in *E.H.R.* lxxix, (1964).

25   *Returns relating to power looms used in factories for the manufacture of woolens, cotton, silk and linen respectively, in each county of the United Kingdom respectively, so far as can be collected from the returns of the factory commissioners*, p. 9, H.C., 1836 (24) xlv, 145.

26   *Hand loom weavers report*, p. 659.

27   *R.I.F.*, 1850, p. 10.

28   *R.I.F.*, 1857, p. 16.

29   *F.I.R., October 31 1862*, p.65, H.C., 1863 [3076] xviii. 437.

30   *Malcomson Memoir; Hand loom weavers report*, p. 659.

31   D.A. Farnie, *The English cotton industry and the world market 1815–1896* (Oxford, 1979), p.297.

32   *R.I.F.*, 1857, p. 16,

33   *R.I.F.*, 1857, p.16.

34   *R.I.F.*, 1862, p.19,

35   *R.I.F.*, 1867–68, p.23.

36   M Blaug, 'The Lancashire cotton industry,' in *E.H.R.* xiii (1961), p. 366.

37   V.A.C. Gatrell, 'Labour, power and the size of firms in Lancashire cotton in the second quarter of the nineteenth century', in *E.H.R.*, xxx (1977), pp 97–8.

THE WORLD OF THE FACTORY:
PERSONNEL AND MARKETS

1   Michael Winstanley, 'The factory workforce', in Mary B. Rose (ed.), *The Lancashire cotton industry; a history since 1700*, (Preston, 1996), pp 123–7.

2   *W.M.*, 28 June 1856.

3   *W.M.*, 22 January 1876.

4   *W.M.*, 28 June 1856.

5   *W.M.*, 24 November 1865.

6   Cohen, *Tullylish*, p. 163.

7   *Reports of the assistant hand loom commissioners on hand loom weavers in several districts of England, Scotland, Ireland and continental Europe*, 1839–40, p. 659, H.C., 1840 (43–II), xxiii. (hereafter *Hand loom report*).

8   V.O., Field survey, p. 1.

9   *F.I.R.*, p. 59, H.C. 1850, [1141], xxiii, 181.

10   *F.I.R.*, p. 59.

11   *F.I.R., July-December 1842*, p.14, H.C. 1843, [429] xxvii. 289.

12   *F.I.R., July-December 1843*, p.10, H.C. 1844 [524] xxviii. 533.

13   *Limerick Reporter and Tipperary Vindicator*, 9 August 1867.

14   Richard Lalor Sheil, *Sketches, legal and political*, p. 359.

15   *Waterford News*, 2 April 1869.

16   W.M., 21 August 1871.

17   N.A., Business records, Waterford 8.

18   *Malcomson Memoir.*

19   Inglis, *Ireland in 1834*, i, p. 70.

20   *Waterford Chronicle*, 7 December 1839.

21   *F.I.R.*, May-October 1849, p. 59, H.C. 1850, [1141], xxiii, 181.

22   *Report from the select committee appointed to inquire into the postal arrangements in the city and county of Waterford, and counties of Tipperary, Cork and Limerick; with the proceedings, minutes of evidence, appendix and index*, 1854–55, p. 41, H.C. (445) xi, 297.

23   *W.M.*, 28 June 1856.

24   *Hand loom report*, p .569.

25   *W.M.*, 26 October 1858.

26   *W.M.*, 26 October 1858.

27   *A return of average weekly earnings of agricultural labourers in Ireland, for the six months previous to 1 January 1861*, p. 7, H.C. 1862, lx.

28   *Census of Ireland, 1841*, p. 248.

29   *Census of Ireland, 1861*, pt 1: p. 248.

30   *R.I.F.*, p. 3, H.C. 1836 (138), xiv, 51 (data collected in 1835).

31   *R.I.F.*, p. 16, H.C. 1857, Session 1 (7), xiv, 173 (data collected in 1856).

32 *R.I.F.*, p. 335, H.C. 1839 (41), xlii, 1, (data collected in 1838).

33 *R.I.F.*, p. 335, H.C. 1839 (41), xlii, 1.

34 *R.I.F.*, p. 16, H.C. 1857.

35 *R.I.F.*, p. 19, H.C. 1862 (23), lv, 629.

36 *R.I.F.*, p. 23, H.C. 1867–8 (453), lxiv, 811.

37 *R.I.F.*, p. 71, H.C. 1871 (440), lxii, 105, (data collected in 1870)

38 *R.I.F.*, p. 7, H.C. 1875 (393), lxxi, 57, (data collected in 1875).

39 Michael Winstanley, in 'The factory workforce', in Rose (ed), *The Lancashire cotton industry* p.124.

40 *R.I.F.*, p. 3, H.C. 1836, (138), xlv. 51.

41 *R.I.F.*, p. 335, H.C. 1839, (41), xlii. 1.

42 *R.I.F.*, p. 335, 1838.

43 *An act to regulate the labour of children and young persons in the mills and factories of the United Kingdom,* 3 & 4 William IV, c.103 (1833).

44 *F.I.R., for half year ending June 30, 1839.* p. 20, 1839 [201] xix, 539.

45 Lewis, *Topographical dictionary of Ireland*, ii, p. 46.

46 *Waterford Chronicle*, 8 October 1839.

47 *R.I.F.*, p. 8, H.C. 1847 (294) xivi, 209.

48 *R.I.F.*, p. 10, H.C. 1850 (745), xlii, 455.

49 *R.I.F.*, p. 16, 1856.

50 *R.I.F.*, p. 19, 1862.

51 *R.I.F.*, p. 23, 1867.

52 *R.I.F.*, p. 71, 1871

53 *R.I.F.*, p. 7, 1875.

54 *The Waterford News* 5 December 1862; Valuation lists number 8, county of Waterford, county health district of Waterford, electoral division of Portlaw, Carrick-on-Suir, number 2, 1855–68.

55 *R.I.F.*, p.23, 1867–8.

56 *R.I.F.*, p. 71, 1871.

57 A Marmion, *The ancient and modern history of the maritime ports of Ireland*, (London, 1858), p. 558.

58 *Hand loom weavers report*, p. 659.

59 Lewis, *Topographical dictionary of Ireland*, ii, p. 466.

60 J.F. Maguire, *The industrial movement in Ireland as illustrated by the National Exhibition of 1852*, (London, 1853), p. 164.

61 David Dickson, 'Aspects of the rise and decline of the Irish cotton industry', in L.M. Cullen and T. C. Smout (ed), *Comparative aspects of Scottish and Irish social and economic history*, 1660–1900, (Edinburgh, 1978), p. 110.

62 N.L.I., Articles of association of the Waterford commercial steam navigation company. Ms.11,978.

63 *Malcomson Memoir.*

64 *Limerick Reporter and Tipperary Vindicator*, 16 June 1865.

65 N.A., Register of ships, 1845–55, revenue I, Waterford; Register of ships, 1855–77, revenue II, Waterford.

66 *R.I.F.*, 1862, p. 19.

67 *R.I.F.*, 1867–8, p. 23.

68 *W. M.*, 6 October 1862.

69 *W.M.*, 30 September 1864.

70 *W.M.*, 6 November 1865.

71 *Munster Express*, 7 October 1865.

72 *Munster Express*, 3 June 1864.

73 *Census of Ireland, 1871*, pt. 1, [C–873–VI], pp 946–52, H.C. 1873, lxii, 119.

74 *Census of Ireland, 1871*, p. 948.

75 *Census of Ireland, 1871*, p. 952.

76 Personal communication from Brenda Collins, Irish Linen Centre, 15 May 1999.

77 *Waterford Newsletter,* 1869–76.

78 P.R.O.N.I., Brett L'Estrange papers, D1905/2/27/6.

79 D.A. Farnie, *The English cotton industry and the world market, 1815–1896*, (Oxford, 1979), pp 171–3.

80 N.A., Malcomson family papers, 975/14/7–9.

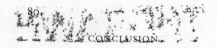
1 *Census of Ireland, 1871*, pp 946–952.
2 Joel Mokyr, *Why Ireland starved: a quantitative and analytical history of the Irish economy, 1800–1850*, (London, 1985), p.176.
3 Graham and Proudfoot, *Urban improvement*, p. 1.
4 *Waterford Mail*, 5 October 1871.
5 David Burns Windsor, *The Quaker enterprise, friends in business*, (London, 1980), p. 170.
6 *The Missionary Herald*, 1 March 1900.
7 *The Missionary Herald*, 1 March 1900.